DATE		

JACK KEROUAC, PROPHET OF THE NEW ROMANTICISM

JACK KEROUAC
Prophet of the New Romanticism

A Critical Study of the Published Works
of Kerouac and a Comparison of Them
to Those of J. D. Salinger, James Purdy,
John Knowles, and Ken Kesey

ROBERT A. HIPKISS

THE REGENTS PRESS OF KANSAS
Lawrence

Library of Congress Cataloging in Publication Data

Hipkiss, Robert A.   1935-
Jack Kerouac, prophet of the new romanticism.

Includes bibliographical references and index.
1. Kerouac, John, 1922-1969. I. Title.
PS3521.E735Z67   813'.5'4 [B]   76-14817
ISBN 0-7006-0151-1

Preface

IN 1957 CRITICS IMMEDIATELY HAILED Jack Kerouac's
On the Road as a major novel about the experience of the Beat
Generation, that generation of disaffected young people who
had come to majority during and shortly after World War II.
While the Beats were making the middle class uneasy with
their use of drugs, with their scornful attitude toward regular
employment and the pursuit of a money-making career, and
with their supposedly promiscuous sexuality, Kerouac, John
Clellon Holmes, Allen Ginsberg, Michael McClure, Gregory
Corso, Philip Lamantia, Lawrence Ferlinghetti, and a number
of other writers and poets based in New York and San Francisco were busy living and transcribing the scene. But it was
Kerouac who captured best the essential, driving desperation
that motivated Beat behavior.

He went on to write novels about the Beat quest for meaning and place in a seemingly mad universe, becoming more
despairing of man's future in the world and concomitantly
more attracted to mysticism. Because the Beat quest was his
own quest, because he was so quintessentially Beat himself,
Kerouac's novels *On the Road, Dharma Bums, The Subterraneans,* and *Big Sur* remain as living testimony to the *angst*
of the lost generation of World War II.

When Jack Kerouac died of drink and self-abuse in 1969,

he brought the desperate vision of the Beats to its inevitable end. Unable to accept life on its own terms and finding no compromise between his own Edenic vision of what it should have been and what it inescapably was, the projector of the vision dissipated his great energies and died.

The vision itself, however, is still very much alive. Kerouac still has a hold on the imagination and curiosity of the young. Any bookstore in any sizable Bohemian cultural center is apt to have paperback editions of his Beat novels for sale, and some may also have his novels of childhood in Lowell, Massachusetts. Colleges and universities throughout the country still use the Beat novels in some of their courses, and students still buy them for leisure reading.

Because the vision of this "prophet," as Allen Ginsberg and Ken Kesey have called him, has not waned even with his passing, we must assume that there is something lasting in it. It is time some careful consideration was given to Kerouac's work for the purpose of finding out what the nature of the vision is.

It is, then, the intent of this critical study of Kerouac's published works to discover the essential themes, the nature of their treatment, and the reasons for their development. The first six chapters are concerned with these matters.

In the first chapter we shall examine the author's development of the child's innocent vision of the world, against which he subsequently measures its reality. In chapter two mother and father images are examined to discover what effects the parents had on the social and sexual attitudes of the focal characters. In both of these chapters, because of the autobiographical and confessional nature of Kerouac's work, we will be looking at members of the Kerouac family as well as analyzing the characters in his fiction.

In the third chapter the *On the Road* quest for heroism and ecstasy is analyzed to determine what promotes it and why it necessarily leads to failure. The fourth chapter scrutinizes the relationship between the Beat hero and nature, on the one hand, and the hero and society, on the other, to see why he is forced to accept "lostness forever."

Having shown the nature of the hero's Romantic vision, the impossibility of its actualization, and the steadfast refusal of the hero to come to terms with the laws of nature and the customs of society, this study in chapter five examines the religious belief that Kerouac and his heroes came to. Its Catholic and Buddhist roots are discussed and so is the Kerouac-Duluoz failure to find it satisfying.

The following chapter discusses the strengths and weaknesses of Kerouac's innovative prose style and traces its roots into jazz and the work of certain contemporary poets.

In chapter seven we shall attempt to set Kerouac in perspective among the postwar Romantic writers by examining the work of four authors who represent different points of view concerning the problems of how to effect love and self-realization in our technologized, nuclear age. Appropriate comparisons and distinctions will be made between Kerouac's work and that of J. D. Salinger, James Purdy, John Knowles, and Ken Kesey.

At this point we will be able to conclude, in the final chapter, just what the Duluoz Legend, as Kerouac called his set of novels, shows Kerouac's prophetic vision to be, the extent to which it is viable, and the degree to which it characterizes the Romanticism of our time.

Acknowledgments

THE AUTHOR wishes to thank Allen Ginsberg and the U.C.L.A. and Columbia University Departments of Special Collections for their assistance in providing materials for his research.

Contents

1

The Child's Innocent Vision

IN THE PREFACE to *Big Sur* (1961) Jack Kerouac says that all of his books are just chapters in a kind of Proustian comedy that he privately calls the Duluoz Legend. He claims that it was after reading *The Forsyte Saga* in a bunk aboard a merchant ship bound for Liverpool in 1943 that he conceived the Legend.[1] Presumably from that point forward he was the self-conscious observer of his own life, determined to record it experience by experience in a string of books until his death. The books are related to one another by having many of the same characters in each of them, although his publishers insisted they be called by different names from book to book. Nearly all the characters have real-life prototypes, and nearly all the happenings in his novels are closely based on fact. Above all, Kerouac's work is united in being the composite expression of his vision, with himself at the center as both actor in the scene and observer of it.

Kerouac's contemporary, John Clellon Holmes, dubbed him "The Great Rememberer." Like Thomas Wolfe, the American author of the late twenties and thirties, whom Kerouac regarded as one of the giants of American literature, one of Kerouac's great strengths is his ability to recall events in graphic detail and to write of them with a kind of desperate verve, "redeeming life from darkness."[2] Time is always Kerouac's enemy, and it is to freeze that enemy in its tracks that he writes, that he makes of his memories a concrete realization that will not change.

In the novels about childhood and the town of Lowell, Massachusetts, Kerouac's tone is, according to one critic, "softer, elegiac . . . and less precisely detailed than in the road novels."[3] These novels, which include *The Town and the City* (1950), *Doctor Sax* (1959), *Maggie Cassidy* (1959), *Visions of Gerard* (1960), and, much later, the book that is largely a reworking of the material in *The Town and the City, Vanity of Duluoz* (1968), were all written some time after the events they describe, unlike the road novels—*On the Road* (1957), *Visions of Cody* (1959), *The Subterraneans* (1958), *Tristessa* (1960), *The Dharma Bums* (1958), and *Big Sur* (1962)—which were written almost immediately after the events recorded. The Lowell novels, as Bruce Cook calls them, are "less precisely detailed" because of the distance between the event and the writing of it. They are also the most sentimental and the most rueful of his novels. They celebrate a child's vision of innocence that cannot come again but which Kerouac desperately holds onto as the only true vision of purity and goodness in a corrupt world.

The most imaginative of these works is *Doctor Sax*, which depicts the world of Lowell's woods and the river as seen by a boy whose mind is alive with the Biblical images of Catholicism and the fantastic characters of *Shadow* comics. Kerouac wrote most of the book in William Burroughs's apartment in Mexico City in 1952 while high on benzedrine and marijuana, which may well account for the heightened, kaleidoscopic imagery of the novel.[4] In no other Kerouac work is childhood so joyous and the impending world of adulthood so foreboding. Where memory fails, imagination takes over, and just as a boy's world is naturally part fact and part fancy, so is the world of young Jack Duluoz.

Speaking of Jack's birth, Kerouac imagines the infant coming into the world aware that he is entering the struggle between good and evil still in touch with the primordial, eternal force (the river) from which life springs: "All eyes I came hearing the river's bed. I remember that afternoon, I perceived it through beads hanging in a door and through lace curtains and glass of a universal sad lost redness of mortal damnation. . . ."[5] The river's endless flowing and unseizable power is a source of awe and trepidation for Kerouac in such passages as this one and in the account of a man's death on the Moody Street bridge, where the child, Jackie Duluoz, says, "I look down with him and there is the moon on the shiny froth and rocks, there is the long eternity we have been seeking" (p. 128).

As he grows older, Doctor Sax, young Jack's mystic mentor, explains to the boy in half-poetic, half Kerouac-Jabberwocky language the pains and delights of adult life but concludes, "you'll never be as happy as you are now in your quiltish innocent book-devouring boyhood immortal night," referring to Jack's nights in bed with the books that arouse his child's imagination (p. 203). The dire warning behind these words is simply that no matter what happens, the adult world will never measure up to the innocent vision of childhood.

The question Kerouac poses for us in so much of his fiction is posed centrally here in *Doctor Sax:* How is it possible to prolong a belief in purity and goodness beyond childhood into the adult world? Doctor Sax suggests that evil is really an illusion, that the snake of evil will be found to be merely a husk of seminal gray doves which will eventually fly apart to reveal the snake's unreality. However, after all of Sax's hocus-pocus the snake proves to be very real indeed and is eliminated only by the coming of a great bird that carries it away in its beak. Jack Duluoz draws the conclusion that the universe counteracts its own evil, and Sax is left standing by the snake's pit, looking rather like a forlorn child whose fondest dreams of personal prowess have just been exploded for all time.

The book may be read as a religious reconciliation. In the beginning of the novel Jack says, "I gave up the church to ease my horrors—too much candlelight, too much wax" (p. 66). Passing by a religious grotto with twelve altars, Jack is reminded of death; but later, after the bird has carried off the snake, he passes the grotto and sees some French-Canadian women there praying, and he puts a rose in his hair, a symbolic acceptance of death, immortality, and Christ's passion (pp. 126 and 245).

The realization is similar to that which appears in *Lonesome Traveler* (1960), where Jack, after looking at a magnificent statue of the crucified Christ and praying, hears the roaring silence of "Purity (which is Divine)." Out on the street he thinks, "Everything is perfect on the street again, the world is permeated with roses of happiness all the time, but none of us know it. The happiness consists in realizing that it is all a great strange dream."[6] The meaning of life is beyond human ken; it is enough to know that there is some internal principle that harmonizes it and balances out the evil in it. It is the belief in this internal principle that enables Kerouac to construct a bridge from childhood into adulthood in the Lowell novels.

In the road novels the bridge is broken, however, and faith is never what it was in childhood. In *On the Road* (1957) Sal Paradise looks backward and says, "The one thing that we yearn for in our living days, that makes us sigh and groan and undergo sweet nauseas of all kinds, is the remembrance of some lost bliss that was probably experienced in the womb and can only be reproduced (though we hate to admit it) in death."[7] In *Tristessa* (1960) he would say, "If only I had the magic self of babyhood when I remembered what it was like before I was born, I wouldn't worry about death now. . . ."[8] As with the romantic perception of William Wordsworth, the child's intuition is superior to the adult's knowledge.

Kerouac's novels of childhood are the ones that express the easiest faith. In his first novel, *The Town and the City*, Peter Martin soliloquizes after a quarrel with his father: "And yet that children and fathers should have a notion in their souls that there must be a way, an authority, a great knowledge, a vision, a view of life, a proper manner, an order in all the disorder and sadness of the world—that alone must be God in men. . . . The *should-be* in their souls powerfully prevailed, that was mightily so."[9] For the saintly brother, Gerard, who died when Jack was four, Kerouac sees that it must have been easy for him to commune with God. In one scene in *Visions of Gerard* (1963), after Gerard confesses to the priest, he hears a roaring silence and feels ecstatic grace: "The heaven heard sound for sure, hard as a diamond, empty as a diamond, bright as a diamond—Like unceasing compassion its continual near-at-hand sea-wash and solace, some subtle solace intended to teach some subtler reward than the one we've printed and that for which the architects raised."[10]

In the preface to *Lonesome Traveler* Kerouac says he is not actually "beat" at all but a "strange solitary crazy Catholic mystic" (p. vi). Although from 1954 on he was deeply interested in Buddhism, he always seems to have regarded himself as essentially Catholic.[11] His faith was wracked by storms of doubt, but to the end he proclaimed (indeed, at times hysterically) faith in the ultimate goodness and oneness of existence, minimizing life's significance and summing up man's purpose here as the need to experience suffering preparatory to his knowing the Golden Eternity. Kerouac confronted a dissolute America with a childlike vision of innocent goodness triumphant. If evil was not merely a husk of doves, then it would still eventually be destroyed by the superior forces of goodness that had to be triumphant in God's creation.

Dan Wakefield has described Kerouac's basic qualities as "stubborn innocence, idealism (even in disillusionment), respect for family, love of friends, and a kind of romantic nostalgia that is special to Americans. . . ."[12] Just how desperately hard it is to retain faith in the dissolute world of the middle-class adult and the Bohemian drop-out and just how necessary Kerouac felt it was to do so are illustrated again and again in his later novels. In *Desolation Angels* (1965), after drinking heavily with Orlovsky, Ginsberg, and Corso and a couple of girls, Jack looks at the crucifix Corso has given him and thinks, "What would Catholics and Christians say about me wearing the cross to ball and to drink like this?—but what would Jesus say if I went up to him and said, 'May I wear Your cross in this world as it is?' "[13] So long as the cross is a testament of faith, Christ would presumably have to answer positively, if only out of a recognition of the world's need.

The childlike faith in a realm of innocent goodness from which we come and to which we return is projected in typical Romantic fashion in Kerouac's treatment of children, Mexicans, Negroes, hoboes, dope addicts, and unspoiled nature.

Most sentimentalized and prescient of his child heroes is, of course, saintly Gerard. Gerard in many ways resembles J. D. Salinger's Seymour Glass. Both characters represent the infinitely wise older brother who dies young and is made a legend of goodness in the younger brother's mind.[14] For Kerouac, Gerard was all but reincarnated in a succession of cats, the death of each one sorely felt and reminiscent of the original loss of Gerard. The child sensitive, too good, too innocent, too sensitive for this world, is enshrined in *Visions of Gerard*. That type appears earlier as Alex Panos in *The Town and the City* (pp. 135–137).

The saintly child has a counterpart in the saintly primitive. In *On the Road*, as soon as Sal Paradise and Dean Moriarty (Kerouac and Neal Cassady) cross the border into Mexico, life seems more beautiful. The marijuana is stronger, the women easier to come by, and the people live for the pleasures of the day. They even find the smell of dirt and bugs pleasanter in Mexico (p. 296). In *Lonesome Traveler* Kerouac speaks of crossing the border as entering "the Pure Land" with a "fellaheen feeling about life, the timeless gayety of people not involved in great cultural and civilization issues" (p. 22). In *Desolation Angels*, when Jack's mother sees a penitent prostrate before the altar in a Mexican church, she now understands why Jack likes Mexico, because even with the dysentery these people "have heart" (pp. 343–344).

At times Kerouac had a hard time romanticizing the misery he sees. In *Tristessa* he wants to make Mexico seem pas-

toral, innocent, and happy but the evidence confutes him:
"Everything is so poor in Mexico, people are poor, and yet
everything they do is happy and carefree, no matter what it is
—Tristessa is a junkey and she goes about it skinny and carefree, where an American would be gloomy—But she coughs
and complains all day, and by same law, at intervals, the cat
explodes into furious scratching that doesn't help. . ." (p. 37).
To save this theme he must minister to Tristessa's condition
with a dose of innocent faith: ". . . holy Tristessa will not be
cause of further rebirth and will go straight to her God and
He will recompense her multi-billionfold in aeons and aeons
of dead Karma time" (pp. 28–29).

Norman Podhoretz, in his castigation of the Beats entitled
"The Know-Nothing Bohemians," notes that in Kerouac, Negroes and whites mingle fully without animosity and that there
is "positive adulation" for the Negro.[15] The reason for the
adulation is, as Sal Paradise says in On the Road, "the best the
white world had offered was not enough ecstasy for me, not
enough life, joy, kicks, darkness, music, not enought night. . . .
I wished I were a Denver Mexican, or even a poor overworked
Jap, anything but what I was so drearily, a 'white man' disillusioned." The Negroes, on the other hand, do not suffer
from "white ambitions" and are the "true-hearted, ecstatic Negroes of America" (p. 180). The adulation of the so-called
primitive is the obverse of the civilized lament. Those who can
be true-hearted and respond to their immediate feelings are
those who do not worry about impressions, those who are not
frustrated writers, those who are not rugged individualists
"hustling forever for a buck among themselves," and those who
do not share the civilized man's responsibility for mechanized
warfare and neglect of the impoverished.

In one of his sketches of street life Kerouac speaks of "the
strangely humble almost clownish position of the American
Negro . . . which he himself needs and wants because of a
primarily meek sweet Myshkin like saintliness mixed with the
primitive anger in his blood."[16] Throughout his fiction, the

Negro is put-upon, a bit of a clown in his ability to see the humor of his situation, and almost never angry. Anger would, of course, humanize the Negro and destroy his enviable (by Kerouac's lights) saintly self-possession and refusal to give this world credit for being as important as the white man makes it.

Kerouac's idealized picture of the Negro becomes downright silly in *Pic* (1971), which is a kind of idyllic children's story, a tale of two brothers crossing the country to "Californy." Nothing destroys the primitive joy in the characters. When Slim is aching all over from shoveling fudge at a break-neck pace in a cookie factory, his response is recorded by his young brother, Pic, as follows: "One time he said 'Ow!' and one time he said 'Whee!' and another time I heard him say 'Oh Lord a mercy, I'll never eat a cookie again.' "[17] This episode is the closest we ever get to anger and frustration in the characters. Arriving in "Californy," they are rather Freudianly rewarded by Sheila, Slim's wife, with a cherry banana split in the Promised Land.

The Negro's lack of inhibition and his joy in human contact never cease to amaze the essentially inhibited and introverted Kerouac. In "October in the Railroad Earth" he speaks for example of "the Negro the essential American out there always finding his solace his meaning in the fellaheen street and not in abstract morality and even when he has a church you see the pastor out front bowing to the ladies on the make . . . his great vibrant voice on the Sunday afternoon sidewalk full of sexual vibratos saying, 'Why yes, Mam but de gospel do say that man was born of woman's womb—' "[18]

Kerouac's most serious treatment of the radical theme appears in *The Subterraneans* (1958). This is the story of Kerouac's own affair with a black girl and exposes most fully the attraction and repulsion that Kerouac felt toward both blacks and women. Critic William Russell points out that the hero, Leo Percepied, drives Mardou Fox (the Negress) to infidelity "because he expects it of her; it is part of an almost unconscious racial stereotype outlook."[19] Leo fears Mardou's insanity (she is schizoid) and her being Negro, fearing she is out to steal his white heart, "a Negress sneaking in the world sneaking the holy white men for sacrificial rituals later when they'll be roasted and roiled."[20] However, the black anger sensed by the hero is sensed so subtly that he cannot be sure whether the Negress hates him or if it is just himself who wants her to hate him for his mistrust. Her actions in the book are those of the long-suffering, somewhat mindless, fellaheen who has learned to live life without expectation and with fatalistic acceptance. In short, it is Leo Percepied who goes against the stereotype of the insensitive white man, not Mardou who undoes the stereotype of the patiently suffering Negro.

Kerouac's hoboes tend to be more eccentric than his Negroes, perhaps because he had had more individual contact with them. Yet, they too are heavily romanticized. The "real hobo," he tells us, is one who has "that secret eternal hope you get sleeping in empty boxcars flying up the Salinas Valley in hot January sunshine full of Golden Eternity toward San Jose where mean-looking old bo's 'll look at you from surly lips and offer you something to eat and a drink too—down by the tracks or in the Guadaloupe Creekbottom" (p. 173). Kerouac knew he himself was not really a hobo, since he would eventually settle down on the earnings of his literary output. As always with his primitives, in the city or out, he was on the outside looking in, seeing the reflection of his own desires in imperfectly understood characters whose real lives were unacceptable. Often his stance toward the hoboes and others is similar to that of his early hero, Peter Martin, who, looking at the panoply of life on Times Square, is "horrified," yet because they all share a common humanity, "he could never turn away in disgust and judgment. He could turn away angrily, but he would always come back and look again."[21]

The hobo, however, whether he be an old 'bo who gives him a cigarette in the creekbottom, or one who recites a long tale about man and the snake,[22] is first and foremost a symbol of freedom. According to Kerouac, "There's nothing nobler than to put up with a few inconveniences like snakes and dust for the sake of absolute freedom" (*Traveler*, p. 173). That our increasingly mechanized and standardized age is threatening the hobo's existence and, by extension, the freedom of all who live now is the message of Kerouac's essay "The Vanishing American Hobo" (1960).

The hobo is sacrosanct in great part because of "his idealistic lope to freedom and the hills of holy silence and holy privacy" (*Traveler*, pp. 172–173). It is the hills and fields outside the cities that call forth the innocent goodness of the Mexican field workers, the compassion of the hoboes, and the mystic awareness of Sean Monahan and Japhy Ryder in *Dharma Bums* (1958). Monahan lives a simple life as a carpenter with an unspoiled wife and two children in a shack in the hills east of San Francisco Bay, and Kerouac assures us, "If the Dharma Bums ever get lay brothers in America who live normal lives with wives and children and homes, they will be like Sean Monahan."[23]

The workaday American civilization as a whole suffers by contrast. In *Dharma Bums* a truck driver envies Ray Smith's freedom as a hobo: the driver "had a nice home in Ohio with wife, daughter, Christmas tree, two cars, garage, lawn, lawnmower, but he couldn't enjoy any of it because he really wasn't free" (p. 102). Learning that it is against the law in Riverside to sleep on the river bed irks Ray Smith: "The only alternative to sleeping out, hopping freights, and doing what I wanted, I saw in a vision would be to just sit with a hundred other patients in front of a nice television set in a madhouse, where we could be 'supervised' " (p. 96). Like Henry Miller, Kerouac sees post–World War II America as an "air-conditioned nightmare." The innocent freedom to feel and do as one spontaneously wished was becoming more and more circumscribed. Soon we would all be robots, put through our paces by some strange and distant governmental process, perhaps even told when to die, as Kerouac envisioned in his lone published science fiction piece, "CITYCitycity."[24]

In *Doctor Sax*, when the Merrimac threatens to flood the town, the boys wish that it would rip through the dull, monotonous, adult-dominated daily life of Lowell. When it does, they are shocked at the damage; and then when the waters recede, Kerouac says there was "something that can't possibly come back again in America and history, the gloom of the unaccomplished mudheap civilization when it gets caught with its pants down from a source it long lost contact with . . ." (p. 180). America is in danger of losing contact with the source of its energies in man as well as nature, and the idea that such an event cannot occur again is a dire prediction that the "mudheap civilization" will find a way to permanently repress the natural forces of life, which means not only preventing disorder but also curtailing spontaneity and freedom as well.

Crossing into Mexico, in *On the Road*, Sal and Dean find shawled Indians "had their hands outstretched. They had come down from the back mountains and higher places to hold forth their hands for something they thought civilization could offer, and they never dreamed the sadness and the poor broken delusion of it. They didn't know that a bomb had come that could crack all our bridges and roads and reduce them to jumbles, and we would be as poor as they someday. . . . Our broken Ford, old thirties upgoing American Ford, rattled through them and vanished in dust" (p. 299). The Ford is a symbol of mechanized civilization and of men more powerful than the primitives who worship that symbol. The empty reward that primitives get is the dust settling around them as the Ford moves blindly on down the road.

There are echoes here too of Aldous Huxley's *Brave New World*, in which Ford is a kind of God to the science-ordered society of Mustafa Mond. The automobile is science and the machine. It is also the symbol of a power in man that is ultimately beyond his control. In *Big Sur* Kerouac looks at the wreck of a car that plunged off the narrow white span of bridge high in the sky over his narrow valley as a "terrifying poem about America you could write."[25] The man at the wheel, Dean Moriarty in *On the Road*, is described as "serious and insane at his raving wheel" (p. 299). The future of mechanized civilization is perilous indeed.

Leo Marx, in his book *The Machine in the Garden*, has noted that industrialization and mechanization are consistently regarded in American literature as corrupting influences. They take man away from dependence upon himself to a dependence upon things, they despoil the landscape and make the naturally beautiful a sight of ugliness, and they condition in man a worship of science and logic at the expense of religion and emotion. Kerouac saw the invasion of the machine into the countryside much in the way that Thoreau saw the coming of the railroad in *Walden*, Sherwood Anderson saw the factories springing up in the small town in *Poor White*, and Steinbeck saw the tractoring of bankrupt farms in *Grapes of Wrath*: as the ruin of man's natural, innocent, and health-giving relationship with the elements of earth, air, and water and the end of a pleasant, cooperative relationship with his fellow-man.

By and large, to the innocent, nature is romantic and religious. In Sabinal, working alongside Negroes and Mexicans in the fields, Sal Paradise feels his back begin to ache, "but it was beautiful kneeling and hiding in that earth. If I felt like resting I did, with my face on the pillow of brown moist earth. Birds sang an accompaniment. I thought I had found my life's work" (*Road*, p. 96). Close to nature the most back-breaking work becomes a joy, unlike Slim's experience in the fudge factory in *Pic*. In the Ice Age valleys of Big Sur, even the more disillusioned Jack Duluoz finds there is a "primordial innocence of health and stillness in the wilds" (p. 22). In *Vanity of Duluoz* he says he agrees with Blaise Pascal that "there are perfections in Nature which demonstrate that She is the image of God . . . and imperfections . . . to assure us that She is no more than His image" (p. 177).

The innocent vision that Kerouac projects against the pernicious progress of the adult civilized world is one, then, that capitalizes on the memories of childhood and that finds in childhood imagination the primal source of our hopes and fears. In *Visions of Cody* he speaks of wandering around New York with a copy of Proust in his pocket and says, ". . . as memories are older they're like wine rarer, till if you find a real old memory, one of infancy, not an established often tasted one but a *brand new one!*, it would taste better than the Napoleon brandy Stenhadl himself must have stared at . . . while shaving in front of those Napoleonic cannons. . . ."[26] To keep in touch with the primal feelings, the artist keeps alive the memories of childhood, embellishes them, interprets them, and of them weaves a sail to tack against the wind.

The embellishment takes the form of an extension of the child's vision to the lives of unsophisticated primitives like hoboes and Mexican field hands, as well as the invention of weird, mysterious, doubtful characters like Doctor Sax and his fantastic adversary, Count Condu. The preoccupation is always with the gulf between eternity and time, womb-secure death and hazardous life, between assured goodness and purity in a time of innocence and the contest between good and evil where each force is real and yet difficult to identify. Man's best hope for remaining on the right track is to keep one's emotional responses to life free and instinctive, always remaining in touch with the innocent primal vision of God's saving beneficence at the core of things.

The dangers of this approach—the disillusionment with all worldly things, the loss of identity with one's society, the nihilistic waiting for death—these Kerouac experienced in full measure. They both limited and informed his work, as we shall soon see.

2

Father Death and Mother Earth

THE FATHER AND MOTHER IMAGES in Kerouac indicate a strong fear of the masculine world and a concomitant Oedipal tie to the mother. This repulsion-attraction syndrome has much to do with Kerouac's lifelong preservation of the child's innocent vision as a stay against the sophisticated adult world.

In the 1950s Kerouac was haunted by a recurrent dream of a shrouded stranger tracking him through streets and across the desert. In his *Book of Dreams* he recounts a dream in which "my Shroud approaches—*I know* he'll get me . . . but being a kid I have great potentiality and all the world yet and left to hide in and cover with tracks—Shall I go towards the mysterious old Chalifoux woods beyond where woodstumps I was born in redmorning valleys of life hope?—or sneak back snaky into town?"[1] The Shroud will get him. But before that fatal end, the child in the dream has time to realize the hopes of his birth. The problem is how to do so. He is torn between retreat toward birth and going onward into a corrupt adult existence (sneaking back, snaky, into town). High on marijuana and preoccupied with Buddhist thought, Kerouac had another dream in which his father comes toward him, and in this dream the father is the "Shroudy Traveller." Desperately the now older Jack Kerouac thinks, "I know how to be beyond him now—by not being concerned not believing in life or death, if this can be possible in a humble Pratyeka at this time. . ." (p. 131). What he is trying to avoid in both dreams is his father's life, his father's son's destiny. In one of his other dreams Jack feels as though he is his father, "the big fat man, but frail and pale, but so mysterious and un-Kerouac—but is that me?" (p. 12). The thought is horrifying.

Leo Kerouac died in the spring of 1946. Kerouac wrote *The Town and the City* in the following two years, in part to atone for the wayward behavior of his youth and the disappointments he had caused his father when he dropped out of Columbia, went to sea, and refused to take a steady job.[2] His attitude toward his father at the time was sympathetic, the feelings about their misunderstandings largely regretful, as we see them in Kerouac's treatment of Peter Martin's relationship with his father in *Town and the City*. In the fifties, as Kerouac alternately supported and was supported by his mother and as he kicked around more and more in the hobo-Bohemian world, he thought back over his relationships with Leo Kerouac and always returned to the same harsh truth—that his father's world would always have rejected him. The anger of that rejection, fed by memories of his father's unsympathetic attitude toward his youthful aspirations and discontents, finally found its way into the much harsher portrait of the father that we find in *Vanity of Duluoz*, written in the sixties in the last few years of Jack Kerouac's life.

The father's death left Jack feeling rootless. The father and mother had moved from Lowell to Ozone Park in 1943, and now the head of the family was dead. The gap between them in life became unbreachable in death. At the end of *Town and the City*, as Peter Martin arranges a blanket around his dying father, George Martin's last words are, "That's right, my poor little boy." In saying this the dying George seems to recognize that the young man, barely twenty-one, is not yet ready to go it alone. In *Maggie Cassidy* (written in 1953) Emil Duluoz, the father, says he is disappointed that he and his son have not been closer this year but, "ah dammit son it's a terrible thing not being able to help you but you do understand don't you God's left us all alone in our skins to fare better or worse—hah?"[3] In *Visions of Cody* Kerouac remembers "the brown nights and my father ignoring me again as I now ignore my own boy—and have to, as *he* had to—" (p. 89). In this statement it appears as though Jack is accepting the necessity of growing up privately within our own skins, the essential isolation of each individual life and its own individualized pattern of growth, but it is far more an attempt at acceptance than an actuality. In *Vanity of Duluoz* Kerouac speaks of his father's death as comparable to the death of God: " . . . 'Father, Father, why has thou forsaken me?' for real, the man who gave you hopeful birth is copping out right before your eyes and leaves you flat with the whole problem and burden (your self). . ." (p. 274). Thinking of Buddha's last words, "Be ye lamps unto thyselves," he compares them to Harcourt-Reilly's benediction in T. S. Eliot's *The Cocktail Party*, "work out thy salvation with diligence," and sees both the Buddhist and existentialist answers to the death of the Father-God as carrion comfort (p. 276). Even had the father lived, it is doubtful that he would have been of much help to the son, but his father passing away, almost complacently, is the final, unacceptable rejection.

In *Visions of Gerard* the father, Emil Duluoz, is an energetic man with a sense of the wrongness of things but unable to do anything about it. In *Doctor Sax* Jack dreams of him as "a man in a straw hat hurrying in a redbrick alley of Eternity" (p. 112), and in the 103rd Chorus of *Mexico City Blues* (1959) Kerouac describes his father with his "straw hat, newspaper in pocket,/ Liquor in the breath, barber shopshines,/ . . . the image of Ignorant Man/ Hurrying to his destiny which is Death/ . . . in downtown Lowell/ walking like a cardboard cut/ across the lost lights. . . ."[4] The father is ignorant, empty, as lost in his way as the son is in his. The father escaped knowing the meaninglessness of his existence, however, by playing the game

American society plays, the competitive game of business and money-grubbing, "lost in the eye to eye the game of men in America" (*Gerard*, p. 112). In *Tristessa* the father is dreamt of as a big-thighed man in a railroad smoking car, while the son is outside in the dark with a brakeman's lantern "lumbering in the sad vast mist tracks of life" (p. 7). The father in this case is a complacent bourgeois who again does not know where he is going, whose son is trying to find the "right track" without his father's help or caring.

The competitive nature of his father's world is most upsetting to the young man. Kerouac dropped out of Columbia in his sophomore year, even though he had a promising year ahead in playing football. In football and earlier while running track, Kerouac's Peter Martin had learned the sadness of victory in the "new dark knowledge he now half-understood —that to triumph was also to wreak havoc" (*Town*, p. 63). In *Maggie Cassidy* too the author speaks of the winner "leaving other boys embarrassed to shame" (p. 106). To what end the competitive struggle? Is it worth the cost in the suffering inflicted? These questions are suggested time and again in Kerouac's work, but he steadfastly rejected the social revolutionary ideas of Allen Ginsberg and others of his politically minded friends in New York and San Francisco. In fact he was very pro-McCarthy during the committee hearings on un-American activities in the fifties and said that if he had voted in 1956 he would have voted for Eisenhower. If a change were to come, it would have to be essentially a change of heart. Meanwhile, as he says in *Visions of Cody*, "America made bones of a young boy's face . . . and made his cheeks sink in pallid paste and grew furrows on a marble front and transformed the eager wishfulness into the thicklipped silent wisdom of saying nothing. . .—Ah and nobody cares but the heart in the middle of US that will reappear when the salesmen all die. America's a lonely crockashit" (pp. 90–91).

To keep the adult world at bay, Kerouac retreated into childhood and sought protection from his father's Shroud by holding tight to the apron of Memère, his mother, Gabrielle Ange Kerouac. The mother-figure in Kerouac's stories is the symbol of life, forgiveness, and love just as the father is the specter of death and calloused striving.

In his youth Jack Duluoz was "a little angel of pure future" to his mother. Later, while he was at Horace Mann on a scholarship, his mother was sure that he was to become a big insurance executive (*Cassidy*, p. 164). The mother's faith in him and her protectiveness contrast sharply with the father's disapproval and sporadic interest in his affairs. Her comfortable, earthy solidity was his bulwark against confusion and death, from childhood on. When death came to Gerard, when Jack Kerouac was four years old, he knew the suddennes of loss and the wrenching adjustment of human relationships for the first time. He had always been a little jealous of Gerard, feeling that his mother loved Gerard more than him, and now he sensed the loss of the kindly older child for her as well as for himself (*Gerard*, p. 88). In *Doctor Sax* Kerouac speaks of the mother's uncanny sense of impending death, true in the case of the neighbor, Mr. Marquand, as well as that of her husband, Emil. The death of the neighbor also scared young Jack, but when in a flu epidemic he and his mother were "semiquarantined in [the same] bed for a week," he "conquered death and stored up new life" (p. 148).

In the 237th Chorus of *Mexico City Blues* the author calls his mother "*la terre*," and says that ideal mothers like his own and Damema, mother of Buddha, obey their pure and free impulses and are champions of birth. In other words they are solidly in contact with their instincts and, being creators themselves, they respect creativity in all forms. They are, then, the ideal helpmates to the romantic, creative artists.

When Kerouac looked up his family's coat of arms in the British Museum he found the family motto: "Love, work and suffer" (*Traveler*, p. 171). Memère accepted this dictum not so much because she was a Kerouac but because she was a devout Catholic, so much so that her son says of her in *Deso-*

lation Angels that in a previous lifetime she must surely have been a Head Nun. Memère is in good company. Kerouac places her faith and understanding beside those of Mozart and Blaise Pascal, who knew that man is on earth to suffer and that his vain attempts to know ideologically what is right and necessary to make a Heaven on earth are foolish, prideful sins, doomed only to make earthly life more hellish. Memère, like her son, had no use for revolutionaries (p. 360).

Kerouac refused to accept the notion that he was tied to his mother by a kind of Oedipal attraction. He belittled the Freudian interpretation of their relationship and psychoanalysis in general.[5] In a direct reply to his critics, in *Desolation Angels* he says that after his trips around the country and to Mexico, Tangier, and Europe his mother offers the welcome relief of peace, good sense, and an immaculately kept home (pp. 336–337). For Memère it was *"la tranquillité qui compte!"* She had little use for abstract reasoning and philosophizing in general. What counted was *"fun*, good food, good beds, nothing more" (p. 360). There can be no doubt that she provided a comfortable retreat for the fatigued and disillusioned vagabond.

Nevertheless, Kerouac's attachment to his mother cannot be accepted as merely comfortable. The Freudian implications remain, even though Kerouac tried to dismiss them. The fact of the matter is that his relationship to Memère affected his attitudes toward sex and his relationship with women quite profoundly, and these attitudes and experiences in turn found their way, barely transmuted, into his autobiographical fiction.

In his *Book of Dreams* Kerouac recounts a dream of himself with his mother arm in arm on the floor. He is crying, afraid to die, and "she's blissful and has one leg in pink sexually out between" (p. 123). The mother comforts the son and brings him away from death, but in suggesting its opposite, procreation, she is suggesting what he calls here a "snaky affection," an affection that could lead to damnation, something as bad or worse than death itself. This one dream sequence illustrates quite vividly the Oedipal tie as preservation against death and the father's world. More deeply, however, it also suggests the source of the Duluoz-Kerouac fear of being possessed by the sexual attraction of woman.

Throughout the adventures of his heroes there is an attraction-repulsion oscillation where sex is concerned. The call of the road to Dean Moriarty, Sal Paradise, and Jack Duluoz is as often as not a call away from entanglements with women. Even when the male character expresses a desire to have a healthy sexual relationship with a woman, he inadvertently scares himself into flight. Sal Paradise, for example, thinks of wanting to make love to Rita, to "calm her fears about men." Then he thinks that he would like also to talk to her with "real straight talk about souls," and as soon as that somewhat religious idea intrudes, he hears "the Denver and Rio Grande locomotive howling off to the mountains" and he wants to pursue his star further (*Road*, p. 57). What the road means in sexual terms is well illustrated in his *Playboy* article "Rumbling Rambling Blues" (January 1958) in which Kerouac recounts an adventure on the road. He bought an old Negro a dinner and the Negro sings an old witch doctor's song especially for him. The song tells him to roll like the log and not to get caught on the snag where the witch doctor lies down with the snake. In accordance with the message of the song, Kerouac hits the road again the next morning (pp. 57, 71–72).

The most complete expression of the attraction-repulsion syndrome in his fiction is in *The Subterraneans*. Leo Percepied (the name is close to Oedipus in French) tells us that he is paranoid concerning Mardou Fox, attracted to her without trusting her. Kerouac's friend John Montgomery has suggested that this was Kerouac's case with women in general.[6] Leo treats Mardou rather badly and finally loses her to a twenty-two year old "subterranean jester," Yuri Gligoric (actually Gregory Corso), and when he does he feels great pangs of jealousy. Mardou suggests that Leo needs to emancipate himself from his mother, and he tells her that he is trying hard to

divide his time equally between them. It is obvious that he has
no intention of gaining true emancipation. In fact, by encour-
aging what he knows is a "big subjective fantasy" that his
mother desperately needs him, he can hold back from any lasting involvements with other women.

The women least likely to make demands upon him are
the most desirable in Kerouac's works. In *Tristessa* the girl
Tristessa is a morphine addict like Bull Gaines (William Gar-
ver), with whom Jack is staying, and she is also Gaines's pro-
curer. She lives in a dirty apartment in Mexico City with a
"sister" who is "seek" and a male dope addict, a dove, a Chi-
huahua, a pink cat, and a hen and a rooster. In the summer of
1955 Jack has been reading Buddhist scripture and trying to
live without lust, and now he finds himself attracted to Tristessa's flat-chested body and beautiful thighs. He leaves Mexico
City, having successfully refrained from seducing her but now
more in love with her image than ever.

A few months later Jack completes a year of celibacy
based, as his alter ego, Ray Smith, says in *Dharma Bums*, "on
my feeling that lust was the direct cause of birth which was the
direct cause of suffering and death. . . ." Japhy Ryder (Gary
Snyder) tells Ray Smith that he distrusts any philosophy that
puts down sex and introduces him to Princess, an energetic
practitioner of *yab-yum*, a Buddhist, mystic sex exercise. She
quickly releases Ray Smith from his bond of chastity with her
sexual embrace. In fact she so satisfies Ryder, Smith, and Alvah Goldbrook (Ginsberg) that they all agree that Princess
should be a regular event every Thursday night (pp. 25–26).

Returning to Mexico City in the summer of 1956, Jack
finds Tristessa has suffered a personality change as a result of
taking goof balls. He is more sexually attracted to her than
ever, but she is only interested in making a marriage of con-
venience with Bull Gaines, using his money and her black-
market connections to keep them high on morphine. Fortunately for his male pride, Kerouac discovers that the morphine
has almost completely vitiated both Bull's and Tristessa's sex

drives. Later, Kerouac told his biographer, Ann Charters, that he had actually "nailed" Tristessa this second summer and that "it was certainly justification of Mexico!" To admit having had intercourse with her, though, would have marred his portrait of Tristessa as a kind of fellaheen saint in the book, so he left it out. Charters says, "Jack saw her as a Madonna, too far removed from him in her absorption with her own sickness and death to ever love him. This only enhanced her appeal, since it meant she wouldn't be possessive" (*Kerouac*, p. 225).

It was in his celibate period, in October 1955 as a matter of fact, that Jack was picked up, while hitchhiking, by a blonde in a swimsuit. Although they are both high on benzedrine, they simply roll along listening to jazz and rock and roll until they hit the familiar rail yards of South San Francisco, where he takes his lady's hand and his leave. Kerouac chronicled this modernized version of errant knight and chaste lady in a story for *Playboy* entitled "Good Blonde."[7]

In Kerouac's works most of the major women characters are long-suffering on behalf of their men. They are, in this respect, extensions of Memère. Certainly this is true of Dean Moriarty's several wives and girl friends in *On the Road* and *Big Sur* (where his name changes to Cody Pomeray). It is true also of Sal Paradise's aunt, who always sends him money when he is hard up, and of Terry, the Mexican girl, who takes Sal in for a time in *On the Road*. Women are the caretakers of the earth; as such, a patient endurance is required of them, and a willingness to suffer. The role is archetypal in literature and certainly a part of the female characterization of Wolfe and Hemingway, two of the major influences on Kerouac's writing in the early years.

Woman, however, is also a biological trap. Her overall purpose is procreation, and in order to fulfill her function she must get a male not only to copulate with her but to provide for her and her offspring while the young require constant maternal care. The woman asks the man, then, to be responsible for her and the children at the expense of his own freedom and desire for self glory. In the 201st Chorus of *Mexico City Blues* Kerouac speaks of women as ones who tempt the saints from meditation on "the enormous/ nothingness/ of the skies." Women fill an unholy and very earthly office. Women continue the cycle of karma. The man would escape into pure spirit, becoming a mystic, a hobo will-o'-the-wisp, a Dean Moriarty kind of "holy goof."

A similar attitude toward women is expressed by Kerouac toward one of his first two wives in a dream that Jack Duluoz has in *Desolation Angels*: "I'm a regular fool in pale houses enslaved to lust for women who hate me, they lay their bartering flesh all over the divans, it's one fleshpot—insanity all of it, I should forswear and chew em all out and go hit the clean rail. . ." (p. 42). In his *Book of Dreams* he reports a dream of digging in an old woman's cellar, which seems like a grave, to find a place to stash his marijuana. The old woman and the earth seem closely identified in the dream. The protective place (home) and the protective woman are identified here with stultification and death (p. 9). Yet he also has dreams of failure to make out with wealthy women, and in one of them he steals a pink sweater. "It is the middle class security of pink wool sweaters I wanted," Kerouac tells us (pp. 25–30). And he says in *Desolation Angels* that being a family man "might have been better than what it may be, lonesome unkissed Duluoz lips surling in a tomb" (p. 30).

Throughout his work the power of woman is paramount. It is woman who controls the world in Kerouac's "CITYCity-city," his look into the future.[8] In a story that owes much to Huxley's *Brave New World*, Orwell's *1984*, and the writings of his friend William Burroughs, Kerouac envisions a future civilization, suffering from overpopulation, which is so regulated that people are confined to various zones for three hundred years and then promptly electrocuted. Their lives are controlled by the Computer of Infinite Merit and Master Center Love, which propagandizes them through Multivision, an electronic device attached to their bodies to keep them quiescent. The Master Center World Drugs also provides 17-JX, a drug a bit like Huxley's Soma, which provides a feeling of "polite, courteous loving." Over this highly regulated society rule The Women. The analogy to the world of Kerouac's novels is clear. Women use love as a kind of drug, offering lifelong security to the male, while at the same time giving birth rampantly and overpopulating the world to no particular end. In spite of their power, however, The Women cannot keep some of the men from sniffing a natural spirit substance called Action, which makes the men desire impossible activity. The drug of Love is not enough to make these men quiescent. These "bums" are known as Loveless Brothers.

Such a strongly misogynistic story might be considered as a backhanded plea for homosexuality. Kerouac had a number of acquaintances who were homosexual, among them Burroughs and Ginsberg. Ange and Leo Kerouac warned Jack against his friendship with Allen Ginsberg (who appears as a character in at least seven of his novels). Leo called him "Cockroach." Jack had met Ginsberg at Columbia in 1944 and retained a life-long, if at times uneasy, friendship with him. Ginsberg was interested in Marx, among other writers, in those years and was fairly outspoken. In *On the Road* he appears as the intellectual Carlo Marx. He was also fighting his own homosexual tendencies. By 1955 he was living in homosexual union with Peter Orlovsky in San Francisco. That Ginsberg's homosexuality made Kerouac somewhat uneasy is testified to by a dream recorded in his *Book of Dreams* in which he flees Ginsberg's snakelike arm across his shoulders and is almost immediately rewarded by his mother with gifts (p. 106). There are other dreams too in which Kerouac fears that he may be losing his sex appeal with young women and fears that he might be homosexual. In his work Kerouac shows a patent acceptance of homosexuals, but they are always seen from the standpoint of one who is himself sexually attracted only to women.

In his novels the hero's sexual fantasies vary somewhat,

depending upon what Kerouac was reading and the situation in which the characters find themselves. In *Maggie Cassidy* (written in 1953) the returning merchant seaman calls up the girl he took to the prom at Horace Mann three years before. He is determined now merely to get a "good lay." He tries to copulate with her in the back of a borrowed Buick but he is stopped by her protests and a rubber girdle. The much-admired Maggie is no longer a romantic interest but a sexual frustration. In Part I of *Tristessa*, written during his celibate period, the woman's body is admired from afar and her being is spiritualized. In *Desolation Angels* (written in summer 1961) the sexual fantasy is so much like the expression of frustrated potency in Henry Miller's *Tropic of Capricorn* that it almost defies coincidence. Likewise, this passage from *Visions of Cody*: ". . . I couldn't resist you in church, I'd lick your snowy belly anywhere, in front of any crowds, any time, on the cross . . . , I'd bring you $57.90 a week base pay and let you suck me off by the washing machine . . . , I want to grab your thighs with my two hands and spread them forcibly and I want you to just lie back and watch me. . ." (p. 291). After studying Buddhism for at least five years, Kerouac is also capable of seeing copulation as the kind of spiritual release that the Mahayana Buddhists find in the practice of *yab-yum*, an aspect of Buddhist practice that he finds far more physically gratifying than spiritually uplifting in *Dharma Bums*, which had been written four years earlier. In *Big Sur* (written in October 1961) he speaks of Jack Duluoz lying with Cody's mistress, Billie, "in unbelievable surrendering sweetness so distant from all our mental fearful abstractions it makes you wonder why men have termed God antisexual somehow. . ." (p. 148). Here, for the first time, Kerouac reconciles the necessity of sex with holy propriety. In all the earlier work sex is regarded as a part of man's bestiality and chief sign of his depravity, though its power is never denied.

Looking now at Kerouac's relations with his parents and his attitudes toward women and sex, we can readily see their influence on his preservation of the child's innocent vision. Kerouac identified the father with the heartless, competitive struggle that threw him out of work in the thirties and that blinded him to spiritual and artistic values dear to the feelings of his sensitive son. Kerouac's preservation of the innocent vision, then, is a refusal to enter the world of the father. Just as J. D. Salinger's Holden Caulfield wants to be a "catcher in the rye" who preserves the innocent happiness of little children, so Kerouac too wants to preserve the world of childhood against what Holden calls the "phony crap" of the adult world.

Central to the child's world, however, is the mother, the protectress and comforter. Memère played this role until she became invalided in 1966. That same year the son married a friend since childhood, Stella Sampas, whose unenviable lot was to take care of both Memère and her wayward son until his death in 1969. Although the attraction to a woman's maternalism is strong in Kerouac, so is the desire for action. Like the "Loveless Brothers" of "CITYCitycity," he and his characters feel restless even under the drug of Love. The woman's smothering protectiveness and her management of his life are a frustration to the writer and his heroes when they require that the male assume the role of head of a family in a day-to-day competitive society.

The answer to the onus of female demands is escape, escape into art and escape onto the road. In his writing Kerouac is constantly throwing up a wall against time, the coming of adulthood, and preserving a vision of innocence and spirituality against a sophisticated, Godless world. The greatest threat to his success is entrapment in the world of woman, and the most powerful weapon at a woman's disposal is her sexual attraction. At successive times Kerouac's heroes try to get sex on the run (*Maggie Cassidy*), ignore it altogether (*Tristessa*, Part I), revel in it even if it means setting up housekeeping for a time (*Desolation Angels* and *Visions of Cody*), revile it and revel in guilt because of it (*The Subterraneans*), and, finally, even bring the woman and sex into the man's vision of spirituality (*Big Sur*). This last is a final attempt at reconciliation, of sexual and spiritual need; it does not, of course, do away with the danger of entrapment in the domestic life unless the woman forsakes her archetypal role.

3

The American Hero Quest

IN HIS YOUTH Kerouac was a lonely child. He did have playmates, but a great deal of time was spent by himself making up imaginary games and stories. In *The Town and the City* Mickey Martin, one of his youthful selves in the fictitious Martin family, conducts a whole, perfectly ordered, imaginary "world" of his own. After reading *Huckleberry Finn* he writes his own story, *Mike Martin Explores the Merrimac*. He also writes his own "newspaper," as the youthful Kerouac did, in which all sorts of exploits of sport and adventure, featuring "Mike" Martin, are recorded (*Town*, p. 120). Mickey and his brother Peter take their Catholicism seriously. They see Jesus as heroic on the cross and rejoice in his resurrection, while the people in the pews around them are "indifferently turning away from immortality and heroism, abysmal, empty, and unamazed." The appeal of Christ is an appeal of heroism, and Kerouac says, "They had to be heroes or nothing" (p. 121).

In *Doctor Sax* the boy's world is largely fantasy, with Jack Duluoz as boy-hero and Doctor Sax as his mentor. Sax thinks of himself as protecting the mortals "from horrors they can not know," while "standing now severe and quiet on second base at One A.M." (p. 151). Sax too is childlike in his heroic pose, and he and the boy Jack, and nearly every other Kerouac hero, think of themselves as given special knowledge and a special role, that of protecting the innocent. Jack is so caught up in his visions of Doctor Sax and the struggle with evil that while playing on a raft on the flooded Merrimac he fails to notice that the raft has become untied. Finally, hearing the shouts of his playmates, he jumps to shore at the last minute. His quest for heroism is so strong, however, that rather than feel fright at the narrow escape he looks at the raft tossing in the main current and thinks it could have been his ship (pp. 170–171).

The drive to heroism is never far beneath the novel's surface of events. In the Lowell novels, in *On the Road*, and in *Visions of Cody*, there is a strong quest for heroism found in action. In fact the central characters seem to be looking endlessly for the event that will make true heroes of them—the predicament to get out of, the brilliant maneuver that will make people gasp in admiration, or the great vision that will solve the problem of unhappiness in this life. In the later novels the heroism sought is a heroism of the spirit, learning to sit quietly, to accept life's vicissitudes, and to love what one cannot understand. Neither heroic quest is successful, of course. Both demand too much for the undisciplined temperaments of the characters.

Even in the most contemplative passages of Kerouac's novels, the answer to the problem at hand is seldom completely grasped. The anguish is not dissipated through rational thought. More often than not it is escaped in flight real or fancied, in which the disturbed character is suddenly distancing himself from the problem with a pell-mell ride in an automobile or a railroad car, or dreams of himself with godlike powers as in the following passage from *Visions of Cody*. After anguishing over his father's death, his mother's taking in boarders, and his own failed marriage, Jack Duluoz ends his soliloquy with: "I may be a distracted wretch but I am still a man and I know how to fight and survive, I have before. Gods, if not help me, if instead barb me, be careful of me, I can catch thunderbolts and pull you down and have done it before. Adieu!" (p. 93).

In *Vanity of Duluoz* Jack does not blame his own lack of realism and logic for his failures. They are inevitably due to what are really great virtues in the romantic view of things, his enormous sensitivity and genius. Gerard was too sensitive for this world and died young; Jack in high school was "too sensitive to all the lunkheads [he] had to deal with" (p. 7). Along with this great sensitivity goes the sort of genius that can read the *Iliad* in three days even though he spent most of his time washing dishes in the cafeteria and scrimmaging on the football field. And, of course, he always has the heroic vision of himself as a great writer. Sensitivity and genius put the self-conceived artist apart from his fellow-man. He is not to be judged by their standards. He is a hero unto himself.

Kerouac's view of the writer as hero parallels his quest for a great American hero for his fiction. He found a model figure in an older brother substitute, Neal Cassady. He first met Neal in 1947 while working on *Town and the City*, and Neal's personality works its way into the fictional older brother in the book. Kerouac's only brother, Gerard, died when Jack was four. Jack is easily identified with Mickey Martin and Peter Martin and to some extent with Joe, but it is Neal he is talking about when he describes Joe as one who always has a job and money, loves girls and cars, has abundant energy, and "never seems to find time to mope or sulk" (*Town*, pp. 9–11). Neal appears in Kerouac's novels after *Town and the City* as Dean Moriarty in *On the Road* and Cody Pomeray in *Dharma Bums, Desolation Angels,* and *Big Sur.* He is also called Cody in Kerouac's *Book of Dreams.*

When Jack Duluoz meets Cody for the first time, two other Columbia University students describe him to Jack as "a mad genius of jails and raw power" (*Cody*, p. 338). Jack Duluoz tells us that Cody was one of seven sons and that like Jack he has sinned against his father (p. 381). His father was an alcoholic, and he and his father hit the road together when Cody was only a boy, only to become separated out West. The father had become dependent on the boy, and Cody feels guilt for his failure to look after him. Duluoz says that Cody never knew his mother. Actually, Neal Cassady, according to his autobiography, *The First Third*, knew her well enough to give us the portrait of a bedraggled housewife who was simply overwhelmed by her several children and drunken husband. Whether he "knew" her or not, it is certain that she was unable to give Neal the affection the young boy craved. He began stealing cars and went through a succession of reform schools, where he became an omnivorous reader despite only sporadic schooling. At reform school he developed athletic prowess. His sexual prowess he learned in the gutter. Upon release from the reformatory, as soon as he had taken a job somewhere and had a little money in his jeans, he would grab a car and a girl, venting his energies in speed and sex. It is apparent from his first novel forward that Kerouac is fascinated by Neal Cassady's penchant for immediate, spontaneous action and rapid-fire talk. As Kerouac got to know him, he was also amazed at Neal's success with women. Further, he came to see Neal as one who was as lost as he and just as desirous of finding the key to life's meaning. In *On the Road* Dean Moriarty makes Sal Paradise think of a lost brother, perhaps the brother Kerouac wished he had (p. 10).

Here was the young American hero that the author had been looking for. Kerouac began to see Neal as an "archetypal American Man."[1] For fictional purposes he dramatized certain events in Neal's life, accenting the horror of his abandoned situation as a child, his fear of losing his father, his fear as a child on the road of a legless beggar's hairy embrace, and the effects of this sort of anxiety on the sensitive psyche of the hero. Describing his early environment, Kerouac says, "This is the bottom of the world, where little raggedy Codys dream, as rich men plan gleaming plastic auditoriums and soaring glass fronts on Park Avenue. . ." (*Cody*, p. 5). Cody is a creature of hope in spite of his circumstances. Cody's dream is one of innocent happiness gotten through spontaneous activity, sex, and love. It is the dream of the child innocent.

Coupled with this vision, Cody (Dean Moriarty in *On the Road*) has "the tremendous energy of a new kind of American saint" (*Road*, p. 39). He has "the face of a great hero—a face to remind you that the infant springs from the great Assyrian bush of a man, not from an eye, an ear or a forehead—the face of a Simón Bolívar, Robert E. Lee, young Whitman, young Melville, a statue in the park, rough and free" (*Cody*, p. 49). He is able to throw an incredibly long football pass and run faster than anyone else. He has great sexual power too, having pushed his father off Cherry Lucy when he was only thirteen. His strength of body is matched by his strength of mind. He reads Schopenhauer, magazines, encyclopedias, etc., etc., and in the reformatory he decided to read, we are told, in order never to be a bum like his father. Kerouac says that this was "the decision of a great idealist" (p. 56).

When Kerouac created Dean Moriarty out of Neal Cassady for his novel *On the Road*, he created a new symbol of flaming American youth, the American hero of the Beat Generation. The book was to have had the title *Beat Generation*, but Kerouac's publisher insisted upon changing it.[2] Kerouac had coined the term "Beat" in 1948 while he and John Clellon Holmes were "trying to think up the meaning of the Lost Generation and the subsequent Existentialism." In 1954 he had a vision in a Catholic church in Lowell, Massachusetts, that told him that the real meaning of "Beat" was Beatific.[3] Kerouac makes Dean Moriarty both "Beat," in the sense of being alienated from the mainstream of American middle-class life, and "Beatific," in the sense of converting alienation into spiritual transcendence.

In *Visions of Cody* his early visions of Neal and himself were "as if Cody and I were construction workers not dissipates who dissipate so much it becomes a principle and finally a philosophy and finally a revelation" (p. 37). He did not realize how Beat they were at first. His hero was to triumph within the society with his manly strength and virtuous idealism. As he shared more and more adventures with Neal Cassady, however, Kerouac began to see that both his hero and himself were too far out of the mainstream for there to be a heroic triumph within it. The triumph would have to be a transcendence of soul. Like Jack's brother, Gerard, Dean Moriarty is in touch with the divine, and his actions that are socially unsanctionable (Gerard's never are) really are manifestations of his spiritual inspiration.

Without parental guidance, without solid religious belief, and without training for a career, the chief guide to a rewarding life for the young is apt to be the haphazard world of random experience. Sal Paradise and Dean Moriarty have a great thirst for experience, but for them experience is only a prelude to ecstasy. Kerouac himself says that "the only people for me are the mad ones, the ones who are mad to live, mad to talk, mad to be saved, desirous of everything at the same time" (p. 8). It is, of course, an old philosophical premise that the mad are closer to God than the sane, and Kerouac seems intuitively to believe this. He himself was released from the navy as schizoid in World War II. In *Town and the City* the most cerebral of the Martin brothers, Francis, suddenly realized that madness is "the only key to uninterrupted, unobstructed happiness" (p. 322). In *On the Road* experience for Dean Moriarty and Sal Paradise must be intensified to produce the ecstatic "flash" that erases one's rational preoccupations with this world and gives him a sense of oneness with the All-Knowing God.

In order to create ecstasy out of everyday experience, Dean and Sal rush their perceptions together. They are frantic to cram it all in, barely tasting what they devour, but certain that if they do manage to devour it all they will know powerfully and completely what life is. Their enemies are Time and Death. In *Desolation Angels* Cody exclaims, "It's all TIME, m'boy! . . . There's no end to the things to be done! . . . If we only had TIME!" (p. 156). In *Visions of Cody* he is described as being afraid of death—"out of the corner of his eye he talks about danger and death all the time" (p. 298). Death caught up with both of them early. Neal Cassady died young (4 February 1968) of apparent heart failure.[4] They had fairly well burned themselves out in their twenties and early thirties in their frantic search for ecstasy. In *Satori in Paris* Kerouac says that he became a drunk because of his love of ecstasy.[5] The same reason might also be given for the years of drug-taking by both Neal and himself.

Their search for ecstasy naturally led to the exploration of jazz. In his essay "The Origins of the Beat Generation" Kerouac says that between 1944 and 1948 the hipsters and bop were the modern expression of feeling. The Beats were an outgrowth of the hipsters and were about half "cool" and half "hot."[6] The Beats carried forward the hipster interest in jazz and the bop refusal to verbalize in standard, coherent form. Dean and Sal find in jazz a communicable feeling without words that is close to sanctity. In *Mexico City Blues* Charlie Parker, the great horn player, is said to be as musically important as Beethoven (Choruses 239–241). In *On the Road* (p. 206) Kerouac does as good a job as any jazz critic in describing what the soloist can achieve:

> Here's a guy and everybody's there, right? Up to him to put down what's on everybody's mind. He starts the first chorus, then lines up his ideas . . . and then he rises to his fate and has to blow equal to it. All of a sudden somewhere in the middle of the chorus he *gets it*. . . . Time stops. He's filling empty space with the substance of our lives, confessions of his bellybottom strain, remembrance of ideas, rehashes of old blowing. He has to blow across bridges and come back and do it with such infinite feeling soul-exploratory for the tune of the moment that everybody knows it's not the tune that counts but IT—"

"It" is "the moment when you know all and everything is decided forever" (*Road*, p. 129). "It" is a mystical kind of knowing, really quite inexpressible in words. Speaking of visiting a jazz club in San Francisco, Kerouac says, "the only truth is music—the only meaning is without meaning—Music blends with the heartbeat universe and we forget the brain beat" (*Desolation*, p. 119). The world of words and logic is antithetical to the world of feeling. True knowing is done with the heart, without words, without inhibition.

Norman Mailer has connected "It" with sexual ecstasy. He says it is "the paradise of limitless energy and perception just beyond the next wave of the next orgasm."[7] Dean Moriarty apparently feels much the same way for "to him sex was the one and holy and important thing in life" (*Road*, p. 4).

For Dean, though, sex is also bound up with women to whom he must feel indispensable. His self-image is heavily wrapped up in a kind of sexual machismo. As Kerouac says of Cody, "He can't stand . . . people fucking when he's not involved" (*Cody*, p. 298).

As the American Romantic poet E. E. Cummings has said, sex ideally is giving and sharing, and Cody gives more than his share with his several wives and mistresses. He even gives sex to his alter ego, Jack Duluoz, by sharing his mistress, Evelyn, with Jack while he is away. A central part of Cody's difficulties lies in his entanglements with women and his conflicting desire to be free and on the road. The same is also true of Kerouac himself and of Sal Paradise and Jack Duluoz. Cody's life on the road is a continuous bouncing back and forth among his women. Women are at the poles of all his journeys. But Jack, who occasionally touches home base with Memère and occasionally gets to first base with some girl, is generally not seeking to perpetuate his female relationships. Sal Paradise says that Dean behaves this way because of his lack of family and home as a child: "Every new girl, every new wife, every new child was an addition to his bleak impoverishment" (*Road*, p. 132).

Ironically, Cody wants others to depend upon him. He very irresponsibly seeks responsibility for women he has lain with and children he has sired. Watching him at work on the railroad, Jack says that Cody wants the men he works with to have full confidence in him. The same is true when Dean (Cody) takes the wheel of a car and powers it around impossible turns that make Sal (Jack) afraid to look. Cody assumes command in a heroic, godlike way, but he exceeds his powers with everything except the automobile, which he usually manages to push to its peak performance and beyond, leaving it a clanking jalopy, no matter what shape it was in when he first took the wheel.

In *On the Road*, in spite of all his love for everyone and his determination that they all will be happier because of him, he deserts Sal in Mexico while he is sick with dysentery. He marries Inez in New York and then goes back to San Francisco to live with Camille, his divorced second wife. One of his girls, Galatea Dunkel, tells him, "It never occurs to you that life is serious and there are people trying to make something decent out of it instead of just goofing all the time!" and Sal suddenly sees Dean as "the HOLY GOOF" (p. 194). His irresponsibility is excusable because of his innocence, his vision of goodness, and his madness for ecstasy. When Camille threw him out earlier, "he no longer cared about anything (as before) but now he also *cared about everything in principle*; that is to say, it was all the same to him and he belonged to the world and there was nothing he could do about it" (p. 188). After Galatea's rejection, "Bitterness, recriminations, advice, morality, sadness—everything was behind him, and ahead of him was the ragged and ecstatic joy of pure being" (p. 195). Once he no longer is permitted to fumble through his responsibilities, the shackles, always loose, are now off completely, and he is ready to hit the road to "dig everything."

Kerouac often speaks of his characters' response to the scene in the jazz vernacular of "digging." To really "dig" jazz is to feel that it speaks to one's own desires and frustrations. In the mood created and in the improvisations of the moment, the melody pulls the hearer along, anticipating his own emotional requirements and opening the tap of his own pent-up feelings, so that he feels them flowing out of him into the music, released, free, and yet given form, with no effort on his part. If the jazz is really "dug," there is a kind of mystical release. One gets "It." But "digging" jazz requires concentration on the music and letting go of one's emotional repressions. If one is then to "dig" the scene rather than music, presumably the same requirements must be met; and in Dean's case and that of Sal Paradise, they seldom are.

On Sal's first trip across America he finds the truck drivers loud and considerate, Des Moines full of beautiful girls, Iowa with lots of ice cream and pie, and Nebraska with the loudest rough-humored farmer he has seen. Because the farmer conforms to his own preconceived stereotype, he thinks of him as the personification of the West. With Dean Moriarty at the wheel, the two of them proceed at such a blinding pace across the country that cities and towns and farmland all blur into one another, and the reader is left with few distinct impressions except for Dean's passion for speed. There is no time for them to concentrate on what is really happening around them. To take the time would be to lose it, they seem to think. Ironically, they are losing it more rapidly and completely as they go along. They are "high" and they are "hip," but they "dig" very little.

They are very much afraid of standing still. Norman Mailer says of the hipster, "Movement is always to be preferred to inaction. In motion a man has a chance. . . ."[8] The "chance" Dean and Sal are after is ecstatic revelation. The Buddhists generally advocate "sitting quietly, doing nothing" to induce these moments of divine release, but Dean's method is also one that has historic parallels. One thinks of the hyperactive mystics of the Middle Ages and the contemporary Holy Roller sect.

In their blind flight in fast cars, high on benzedrine or "tea," they do not really experience the life around them. Rather, they experience the exhilarating danger of roaring through towns down a seemingly endless road where speed is almost an end in itself. The ideal end, of course, is the ultimate ecstatic moment that will reveal all. After that, they will be able, it is hoped, to deal with life with all-knowing awareness, unperturbed, accepting, in complete enjoyment of life no matter what its vicissitudes. Meantime, Dean is busy trying to make it "over every bush and fence and farmhouse and sometimes taking quick dashes to the hills and back without losing a moment's ground" (*Road*, p. 208).

To achieve ecstasy, time must be compressed, made to stand still and yet be so charged with vital energy that the moment of truth can be experienced in all its requisite intensity and completeness. Time is the enemy that must be conquered, and Dean sometimes reaches a stage of frustration when the conquest seems impossible. In such cases he resorts to an easy fatalism: "Ah, but we know time," he says. "Everything takes care of itself. I could close my eyes and this old car would take care of itself" (pp. 158–159). In other words, one cannot really cheat time; time has a pattern that is foreordained and will work itself out. One has only to go along with it and learn from the experience it provides and enlightenment will come along the way. In an attempt to reconcile the two disparate views of time, he says at one point to Sal Paradise, ". . . we know what IT is and we know TIME and we know that everything is really FINE" (p. 208). He rushes along with his bandaged thumb on high, his symbol of wounded potency, and exclaims "Yes, yes!"—an affirmation of how fine life is if one simply "digs" it all the way, no matter what, without end goals and therefore without frustration.

It has already been pointed out that Dean and Sal do not really successfully "dig" the life they so briefly come in contact with on the road. Nevertheless, except for their unwillingness to take the time to experience what they pass through, they do have a predisposition to "dig," in that their attitude toward life is very accepting and without conventional moral considerations. This is particularly true of their sexual affairs. In this respect they are representative Beats. Paul Goodman says that Beat sexuality is generally pretty good because inhibitions are relaxed, there is courage to seek experience, and "since conceit and 'proving' are not major factors, there is affection." He also notes that homosexuality and bisexuality are not regarded as a crucial problem.[9] As Mailer says in "The White Negro," "to swing is to be able to learn, and by learning take a step toward making it, toward creating."[10] Lawrence Lipton in *The Holy Barbarians* says that Beat sexual relations are not only free and tolerant but are that way as part of the Beat's mystic grail quest. As he paints the picture, the Beat is always willing to put up with poverty, opprobrium of the square world, and the frustrations of Bohemian living for the creation of something beautiful, in sexual relations, in painting, poetry, or mystical insight, helped or not by drugs or alcohol.[11]

As Kerouac describes his days on the railroad, he was always running to catch a train, running to throw a switch, running back from a farmer's field with a stolen prune, always running "happy," as he says.[12] The exultation in spontaneous activity is another Beat characteristic that goes along with the acceptance of all experience as valid in the growth of the individual experientially and as a preparation for ecstatic revelation. Spontaneity and acceptance are at the heart of Kerouac's *jeu d'esprit* dialogue for the Beat film *Pull My Daisy* (1959). This film is based on the third act of a play called *The Beat Generation*, which Kerouac wrote in 1957.[13] The film was a joint creation by Ginsberg and Kerouac. The lyrics of the title song, sung by Anita Ellis in the film, celebrate the joy of being free of institutions and creeds. They proclaim the right to be free of any serious intent to make things orderly and prescribed. The action moves from casual conversation about poetry to joyful needling of a sportsmanlike bishop, and then to a spontaneous blowing of jazz and an exit without formality.

At one point in the film, Ginsberg asks the bishop if this is holy or that is holy, if holy is holy, if he is holy. The bishop, laughing, decides to leave to do his holy offices. What Ginsberg is suggesting in needling the bishop is that all things should be accepted as holy. The acceptance of life that the Beats espouse is all-encompassing, Whitmanesque. Ironically, however, it is precisely the lack of discrimination that this attitude demands that produces the ennui, the lassitude, the sense of being sucked down to nothingness that grates on the inmost nerves of the Beat, and of Kerouac. To fail to discriminate is to make everything equally meaningless, so that in fact nothing is individually worth striving for. Instead of "digging everything," the result is that nothing is really "dug," and everything is reduced, underneath all the excited wide-eyed wonder, to tasteless uniformity.

Unbridled nondiscrimination and spontaneity mean unconventional behavior, of course, and the opprobrium of conventional society. Even Jack Duluoz comes to appreciate this fact. In *Desolation Angels* he is very uncomfortable with Simon Darlovsky (Peter Orlovsky), who believes that all we have to do to have brotherly love is do it, act in accord with our immediate, free (and therefore presumably good) instincts anytime, any place, anywhere. It is apparent to Jack that Simon is not spreading brotherly love with his antics, that he is, in fact, needlessly antagonizing the people around him.

Likewise, Cody, with his irresponsible, pointless activity, turns his "Boswell" (Duluoz) against him late in *Visions of Cody*: "Listen, Cody is full of shit; let him go; he is your friend, let him dream; he's not your brother, he's not your father, he's not your Saint Michael, he's a guy, he's married, he works, go sleeping on the other side of the world, go thinking in the great European night" (p. 362). The hero image is wearing thin, and Neal Cassady's "biographer" knows it. In the end, however, even though Cody has left him in Mexico with dysentery while he rushes back to the U.S. to marry one woman and honeymoon with another, faithful Jack Duluoz decides that his hero, being no ordinary mortal, should not be held accountable: "He's an institution by himself. He has the strength of the bourgeois and the lumpenproletariat all at once, he Out-Marxes Marx, he's a lad. . ." (p. 390). By the end of *Visions of Cody*, the "archetypal American Man" is deflated to being just a guy, and then reinflated as a kind of super-hero who is even more than representative of any class, a supreme hero of lower and middle classes alike.

Throughout *Visions of Cody*, and to a lesser degree in *On the Road*, the hero's colossal energies are regarded as both good and evil. Early in the novel, Kerouac says that Cody has the "tremendous energy of a new kind of American saint." Before the novel is concluded, Duluoz has seen Cody's energy exercised in unsaintly ways, as when Cody thrashes a pervert "on rugs in the dark, monstrous huge fuck, Olympian perversities," while Duluoz sits peeking out horrified from the toilet (*Cody*, p. 358). He also recognizes that though they are like brothers, they could kill one another, for Cody is "a raging murderous man" (p. 331). As Thomas Wolfe's George Weber learned at the Oktoberfest in *The Web and the Rock*, vitality is not good in itself. Energy does not predispose one toward sainthood.

Kerouac would have us see Cody as a kind of Nietzschean hero, beyond good and evil. His supreme energies demand that he appropriate other people's property to his own use and that he exploit others in sex and in friendship to express his power in life, his joy in living, and his consummate drive toward ecstasy. He is the most singular hero of the road America has ever had. Mixing the individualism of the freeborn American with that great present-day extension of his freedom, the motor car, he extends himself literally across the continent in all directions. Were he, in fact, able to fathom everything he so fleetingly observes, he could, in Whitman's phrase, "contain multitudes," but the passion for speed sadly balks his attempt to embrace all of life.

In fact, when we look at Cody with his race driver's foot pressing the accelerator into the auto floor, we are looking at the reduction of four-dimensional experience into the one dimension of sheer power. His frustrated potency finds outlet almost purely in speed and sex. When he works, at recapping tires in *Big Sur*, for example, he works at a furious pace, and it is not the work that satisfies him; it is the pace at which he can work. He seems to find no joy at all in building a thing or in doing an intricate job well. He also takes no pleasure in constructing theories or studying anything at any length. We are told that he and Duluoz converse and discuss deep subjects until the wee hours of the morning, but the snatches of conversation that Kerouac gives us are incoherent, hyper-excited fragments of thoughts and emotional assents, dissents, and exclamations. Cody is said to have great insight, and his mind apparently works too fast for immediate articulation; but again Cody's joy comes not in form but in motion, in this case, in the blinding speed of his own barely articulable sensations.

Cody is the will unable to find any suitable form for its proper manifestation. Every form he takes, as lover, husband, father, worker, and traveling companion, quickly blurs into formless speed. He is a hero without form; he is a figure, a symbol, of the primal drive, the Nietzschean Will to Power. He is will without suitable manifestation; why?

That question might be answered by saying simply that everyday American life today offers little opportunity for heroism. Cody was meant to be great, but America did not encourage his study nor appreciate his skill as an athlete. He has been left to become one of the worker-husband-fathers of middle-class America, but his own heroic energies insist upon his rebellion against such stifling mediocrity. This is, however, only a partial answer. To look at Cody as a representative of the Beat Generation is to see him as a very lost young man who has no real confidence that he can ever make it in any role whatever. His father and mother were failures, and he has never held a job long enough to gain any measurable degree of responsibility. He hungers for the security of a maternal wife and for the pride of a man who knows his *métier* as he knows how to drive an automobile, but his own fears of failure hamper his efforts. His speeding dashes down the road are as much flights of panic, the fear of never making it, the fear of losing all the life he has never had, as they are quests for ecstasy, which is itself an escape from fear and the frustrations of desire.

Kerouac's hero is more driven than driver, much more anti-hero than hero. He is not a potential Robert E. Lee, as

Kerouac suggests in the beginning of *Visions of Cody*. He is quintessentially the lost, the wasted soul, the victim, not the hero, of the American dream as it has been realized by the abundant, comfortable, middle class. He is not beatific either, but he is most assuredly Beat. His vaunted energies are due less to his athletic prowess and quick mind than to benzedrine, marijuana, and the gut-grabbing panic within him.

So it is that Kerouac's quest for heroism in the action of one endowed with supernal energies ends in the creation of an anti-hero whose fires energize no great historical event, whose effect on the life of a nation is lost in the vastness of the continent and the inertial mass of society at large. The hero is set apart from the mainstream of society and really never acts upon it, except in childish fits of car stealing and marital irresponsibility. His hero as artist (Sal Paradise and Jack Duluoz) has more effect, as a spokesman for a generation of disaffected young people, but he is unable to convince the larger society of its guilt in the disaffection of its youth and equally unable to persuade them to seek a mystic's way to Godhead. His life serves as no model of goodness with his failed marriages, his living off his mother, and his eventual alcoholism. The central characters are, however, perhaps best judged by their own code, as ones who are at least faithful to the quest for divine understanding. If they fail, and if they are misguided, theirs is nevertheless a vital effort.

4

Accepting Lostness Forever

IN *THE TOWN AND THE CITY* George Martin, the father, notes a change in the younger generation during World
War II: ". . . I guess there must be a kind of new courage
among you. You can take so much and not give a damn and
still go around with that smile. I give you credit for that, all
of you. But you don't *care*. You don't care for your parents
who love you. Something *evil* and awful has happened, there's
nothing but unhappiness everywhere. And the *coldness* of
everybody" (p. 422–423). The generation coming of age just
before and during World War II was in some measure estranged from parents and family and home by having ven-
tured into life beyond the confines of family and community
and finding the outside world more vast, unprincipled, and
more exciting than life could possibly have been in the home
environment. After being away, a son is apt to find the family's love stifling and his father's advice meant for the ears of
a son no longer his. However, what the father sees as a lack
of love for the parents is really a lack of respect for certain
parental values.

By the end of 1945 Kerouac had deserted Columbia, gone
into the navy and been discharged as unfit for military service,
gone to sea with the merchant marine, taken so much benzedrine that he required a stay in the V.A. hospital for thrombo-
phlebitis, been involved in the suicide of an acquaintance who

was homosexual, and been married and separated for the first time. He had also become one of several aspiring writers frequenting the New York apartments of Allen Ginsberg and William Burroughs. His Martin brothers in *Town and the City* and Jack Duluoz in *Vanity of Duluoz* enact these adventures in one form or another. For them and for Kerouac, these experiences amounted to a change of self, such that they could never really "go home again." When the father accuses the son of becoming a bum and letting his friends ruin him, the son knows that the antidote is worse than the poison. He does not want his father's life at any price, and what is ruination to the father is liberation to the son.

Nevertheless, it is a shock to the son to return and find that "there's no neighborhood anymore." This unwelcome knowledge Ginsberg calls Kerouac's first tragic theme.[1] Not only is the son unable to communicate with his parents, but he has no group of intimates at home that he can talk to at great length about common generational problems, friends who might help him reintegrate into hometown life. Many of Kerouac's generation found that friends had gone to war and not come back or had come back only briefly, soon moving away from their parents to work and live elsewhere. In Kerouac's case the family had left his hometown, Lowell, Massachusetts, in 1941 and had moved successively to New Haven and Ozone Park. Of this dislocation he says in *Doctor Sax*, ". . . I judged I was being torn from my mother's womb with each step from Home Lowell into the Unknown . . . a serious lostness that has never repaired itself. . ." (p. 111).

It is this sense of displacement that is the impetus for the travels on the road and for the relations that Sal, Jack, and Dean and Cody have with most people they meet. These chance relationships palliate the loneliness, but they are not anywhere near sufficient compensation for the loss of family and community. For love, for meaning, for purpose, which are all normally supplied through community living, they turned inward to the play of their own overstimulated minds. They are in a situation similar to that of Kerouac's *Pic*, whose story begins, "Ain't nobody loved me like I love myself, cept my mother and she's dead" (p. 1). After time on the road, they tend to think like Pic's brother, Slim, who sees the future as the knowledge that comes from the trial and failure of the westward quest: "Future of the United States was always goin to Californy, and always bouncin back from it, and always will be" (p. 85). In the "bouncin back" there is the realization that the road does not lead to the Promised Land and that to find happiness one is thrust back on one's resources. At the end of *Pic*, Slim has just arrived in California, but he has had enough disappointments to expect to be on the move again.

The Kerouac hero's lack of connection with the needs and feelings of the community is the despair of liberal critics who came of age in the twenties and early thirties. Kenneth Rexroth, speaking of the Beat Generation as a whole, says, "Social disengagement, artistic integrity, voluntary poverty—these are powerful virtues and may pull them through, but they are not the virtues we tried to inculcate—rather they are the exact opposite."[2] Norman Podhoretz says, "The Beat Generation are rebels, all right, but not against anything so sociological and historical as the middle class or capitalism or even respectability. This is the revolt of the spiritually underprivileged and the crippled of soul . . . , young men who can't get outside the morass of self and so construct definitions of feeling that exclude all human beings who manage to live, even miserably, in a world of objects. . . ."[3] These are rebels without a cause, in the view of the sociological critics. The cause is there, however; it is the cause of self. What is being denied is that self-fulfillment can come from alignment of the self with social causes. In *Satori in Paris* Kerouac says, "I want to tell them that we dont all want to become ants contributing to the social body, but individualists each one counting one by one" (p. 47). The Beats simply do not identify sufficiently with any one class or social interest group to make a cause of their needs.

V. S. Pritchett finds that despite their social disengagement the Beat characters of *On the Road* are "all interested deeply and personally in one another, with a sort of detached tenderness," and that there is "a remarkable absence of hatred among the Beat."[4] The characters, even the hard-used women, have a feeling that, alone as they are, all they have for solace really is the sympathy of one another and the bits of experience they can share. On the other hand, they do not hate long or often because they do not have such close, intense, and dependent love relationships that they can care enough to hate when a friend or husband acts irresponsibly. There is seldom much trust to betray; and, if it is betrayed, the character usually has only himself to blame for expecting more of the other person than that person's temperament allows him to supply. So it is that Kerouac wastes few tears on Galatea's disappointment in Dean Moriarty or on Jack Duluoz's sense of betrayal when Cody leaves him in Mexico to nurse his dysentery alone.

This is not to say that Kerouac is at ease with the lack of *caritas* in the contemporary world. He laments the lack of concern over and over again. At a bullfight in Mexico City he sees the bull as skillfully butchered and dying a nauseating death, which makes him think "how everybody dies and nobody's going to care, I felt how awful it is to live just so you can die like a bull trapped in a screaming human ring" (*Traveler*, p. 33). In Brest, while touring Europe, he says, "All the prettiness of tapestries, lands, people:—*worthless* if there is no sympathy—Poets of genius are just decorations on the wall if without the poetry of kindness and Caritas. . . ." He goes on to say that he dislikes Freud for "his cold depreciation of helpless personalities" and that "when you die you will be elevated because you've done no harm" (*Satori*, pp. 88–89). People have a right to be eccentric and should be cared about as they are, not forced into behavior that is "normal" or "sane." One's place in heaven is assured if he has simply done no terrible harm to others. Obliquely, then, Kerouac is blaming the intolerant behavorial prescriptions of our society for its lack of *caritas*, for its tendency to treat people like the bulls who are made to perform for society's enjoyment and who die in anguish unlamented.

In *Visions of Gerard* Jack Duluoz (Ti Jean in this book) has memories of the first four years of his life with his brother as "permeant and gray with the memory of a kindly serious face bending over me and being me and blessing me" (p. 10). This early I-thou relationship with his brother is the ideal caring that we may feel in childhood but lose as we grow older. Preserving the world of childhood as an ideal of the adult, as Kerouac does, means that the adult hero is apt to feel very lost indeed when he must settle for more conditional love relationships. It is always a sad realization in Kerouac's novels that friendship is limited to a few common interests and that at almost any moment the bond can be stretched or parted. In *On the Road*, for example, after listening to jazz with Dean, losing Marylou and finding her again, and feeling the excitement play out to tired disgust, Sal leaves for New York. His leave-taking is sullen: "We were all thinking we'd never see one another again and we didn't care" (p. 178).

Recorded in his *Book of Dreams*, not long after the publication of *Town and the City*, is a dream in which "everybody wants money or earning power from me, the sweetness is gone —Cody has a harried, unpleasant, sullen expression." The dream shifts to someone shooting at him (p. 10). He speaks in *Visions of Cody* of having wasted his Mexico City experience in 1950 on paranoia, and he wonders why he could not have simply gone out and mixed with the people on the scene and gotten to know "the really interesting ones" (p. 42). What stands in his way is mistrust born of the knowledge that his artistic success has set him apart from his friends and that they are not so loving, kind, and unselfish as he might have hoped. He feels that "everything goes away from me . . .—girls, visions, anything, just in the same way and forever." Seeing no hope of change, he says he must "accept lostness forever" (p. 33).

In *The Subterraneans*, written in the fall of 1953, Leo

Percepied says of his lost condition that his virtues "had long
been drowned under years of drugtaking and desiring to die"
(p. 9). The hero partially indicts himself in this novel for his
lack of caring. Sharing his indictment, however, is the society
whose values made the once moral, sensitive genius this way.
Like Henry Miller in *Tropic of Cancer*, he displaces his guilt
for hard-heartedly using other people upon the society that
shaped him.

In *Big Sur* Jack Duluoz tells us few people pick him up
on the road and "No Rides" seems to be a sign of the times
(pp. 46–48). Drunk in the Nepenthe Restaurant, Jack tells a
general eating there of his idea for buddy platoons for guerrilla
warfare. The night before, in the drunken comaraderie of his
friends, he felt they were unbeatable because of their care for
one another (p. 108). The intense "caring" that he so desires
is, however, not sustainable, and its lack in the sober, somber
world of day-to-day leaves him empty and lost.

The quest for ecstasy, discussed in the last chapter, is very
much inspired by the loss of *caritas*. The character's quest is
a rejection of a world in which love is lacking in some respects
and undependable in others. Whether we are looking at Dean
or Cody, or Sal or Jack or Leo Percepied, the predominant
reaction to the frustrations of love in the real world is the same
as the reaction of Kerouac's saintly brother, Gerard. In *Visions
of Gerard* Gerard has found a mouse caught in a trap and
taken it home to nurse it back to health, only to discover one
day that his cat has killed it. When Emil Duluoz, the father,
tells the boy not to be upset, that his cat is merely obeying the
law of the jungle by which all animals and men live, Gerard
pouts and says that to escape the law he will go to Heaven (pp.
21–22). The ideal love of the child innocent is not a love to
be compromised with adult reality. Rather, it is to be secured
through a mystical transport of self into a perfect union with
Being and Godhead.

In *Big Sur*, with the family split up, the home displaced,
the neighborhood gone and all attempts to find again the I-

thou relationship he had with his brother, Gerard, ending in failure, Jack Duluoz stands looking into a mirror at his haggard and awful face "with sorrow you can't even cry for a thing so ugly, so lost, no connection whatever with early perfection and therefore nothing to connect with tears or anything. . ." (p. 8). Like T. S. Eliot's persona in *The Waste Land*, he can "connect nothing with nothing," because he has no continuity with the past, no growth beyond the disillusioned idealism of early childhood.

Unable to establish lasting human relationships, unable to find a tradition of custom and belief that works in the modern world, the author-hero is left with no outward direction in his life. He must accept the *"truth of loneliness,"* as he calls it in *Vanity of Duluoz*, the simple, grave fact that in the last analysis the individual man is ineluctably alone. As he says in the 36th Chorus of *Mexico City Blues*, the void is everywhere and the only direction to go is inward. The "sweet small lake of the mind" is most welcome after enduring the strange reality of the bleak endless world which has "no destination or meaning or center" (*Dreams*, p. 54). It is in the mind that one has freedom to create his own reality. Looking down through the waters of that enchanted "lake," he marvels at the mind's plasticity. He describes the reality of dreams as "so huge and timeless, the events strung out from some intenser center and forming vague distant points only to be found again when centers and universes shall shift in other dreams" (p. 52). Where the world of real objects and obstacles offers frustration, the mind offers possibility and hope.

Unfortunately, though, the mind also tends to mirror and magnify the chaotic and frustrating outward reality. Like Henry Miller in *Tropic of Cancer*, Kerouac sees his own neurotic feelings as the key to the reality of things. "I know," he says in *Visions of Cody*, "that paranoia is the vision of what's happening and psychosis is the hallucinated vision of what's happening, that paranoia is reality, that paranoia is the content of things. . . ." (p. 17). The romantic writer would have us believe that the magnification of an unwholesome reality is not madness but the focus of an unusually sensitive perception of the world, a heightened illumination of its true, horrible nature. It is also, of course, the reaction of a Gerard-like idealist who will not compromise in his demands that life be as he wishes.

That failure to compromise, his unwillingness to accept society's goals, his disillusionment with love and success in the forms they take in the society around him, make the world appear essentially absurd. In a blueslike passage in the 235th chorus of *Mexico City Blues*, he summarizes his situation in the world: "How do I know that I'm dead/ Because I'm alive/ and I got work to do. . . ." It is only the obligations that the self accepts "to do" that make it feel energy-filled and purposeful, but the obligations are painful and not satisfying; all the striving is really a kind of living death. Unlike Robert Frost's celebrated "Stopping by Woods on a Snowy Evening," there is no satisfactory putting aside of the death wish by contemplating the "miles to go before I sleep." But, then, Frost was more accepting of this imperfect world and more sure of the result of his efforts when he wrote that poem than Kerouac ever was.

The society he sought to escape from created its own foolish illusions, such as that of the glamorous movie queen whose supposedly great talent her public admires and willingly supports. Possibly the most satiric sketch he ever wrote concerns Joan Crawford and the making of one of her movies in San Francisco. It is entitled "Joan Rawshanks in the Fog." The aging actress has to undergo several "takes" just to open a door on the street correctly. Meanwhile, police hold up traffic, and the crowds gather to watch her do so under the klieg lights in the fog. The director of this silly enterprise is sucking on a lollypop. As the crowd catches a glimpse of her dissipated countenance under the lights close up, she creates a pang of disgust in them, but they continue to watch all the same.[5] In another sketch, entitled "Seattle Burlesque," he sees that underneath the grease paint of glamorous illusion the performers on stage are merely poor souls "making a living."[6] The illusion that one can really "make it" in this day-to-day world is illusion only, after all.

Jack Duluoz is attracted nevertheless to the illusion of personal greatness. He thinks of himself at Columbia as a great halfback, but then he sees the meaninglessness of the dream, and "It just didnt matter what I did," he says. "I suddenly realized we were all crazy and had nothing to work for except the next meal and the next good sleep" (*Duluoz*, p. 88). In *On the Road* Sal Paradise realizes he would not make a good marital partner for Lucille because he is constantly chasing illusory ideals, and he has nothing to offer anyone except his own confusion (p. 126).

The church offers no refuge either. In *Visions of Cody* he finds that the glass windows of the church "refract NIGHT," that religion has become as absurd as the world itself, "mixing theological verities with today's headlines," leaving Jack to his own thoughts and no place to go except to find his "road" (p. 31).

The "road" leads to San Francisco in 1960, where in *Big Sur* Jack Duluoz enters the city in the hat and waterproof of a fisherman. Here is the Fisher King of the Beats looking for some evidence of basic faith, wandering lost in the American Waste Land. The partying in San Francisco makes him long for solitude and he goes off to Big Sur. There life too seems wasted. There is a dead sea otter in the seaweed. The absurd role of fate is underscored in his finding in his friend's house a dead mouse that he had fed cheese and chocolates to. He had inadvertently left the cover off the rat poison package. And when he goes to the seashore, the waves make a booming meaningless sound, and the creek's babbling sound soon becomes "an endless jabbering of blind nature which doesn't understand anything in the first place." He takes some comfort in the fact that in a billion years the whole place will be covered with silt, but what he desperately wants when sickest with drink and surfeit with his quest is that someone or something really care, but no one and nothing does (p. 113). Nature is neither purposeful nor caring, and the age-old geologic formations of Big Sur seem cold and indifferent entirely to man's fate and to their own.

Much earlier, in *Town and the City*, Mickey Martin hears the roar of the Merrimac and "ponders the wellsprings and sources of his own mysterious life" (p. 3). In *Doctor Sax* young Jack Duluoz looks at the flooding Merrimac and grows dizzy watching its "filthy brown wave crests." He begins to dislike the flood, "to see it as an evil monster bent on devouring everyone—for no special reason" (p. 179). Doctor Sax's gleeful, mocking laugh can be heard in the background. Sax thinks the world's meaning is inscrutable but basically benevolent until his potions do not work on the snake. In the end the boy and Sax both see the bird carry away the snake and conclude that the universe has a way of canceling out its own evil. The workings of nature are indeed mysterious and in part evil. In *Vanity of Duluoz* (1968), written some sixteen years after *Doctor Sax*, nature is fully indicted, as Jack asks, "Who's going to come out and say that the mind of nature is intrinsically insane and vicious forever?" (p. 277).

By 1968 it was apparent to Kerouac that there was no road out of the Waste Land except that offered through mystic contemplation and death. Nature, the impulses of men and the forces of nature, were themselves corrupt and insane. Such being the case, no change of government, no change of economic system, or of group affiliation would give relief. The only final answer would be for man to opt out of nature altogether, to be free of "All the endless conception of living beings/ Gnashing everywhere in Consciousness . . . ," to be free of what he calls "the quivering meat conception," and "safe in heaven dead."[7]

In spite of the death wish, however, there is in Kerouac a strong desire to live, to find a way to cope with the Waste Land situation, to create a life in spite of it all. Necessarily, it would have to be a life that acts as a stay against time, against the "vicious *change* that hurts," as he calls it in *Desolation Angels* (p. 67). Like Aldous Huxley and T. S. Eliot, as he became more and more disenchanted with this "brave new world," and as he read more deeply in the religions of the East, he confirmed his early fears of time's relentless advance. Time's movement is prompted by the chaotic forces of fate and man's endless, short-sighted desiring. To withdraw from the world, to find a stable sameness of routine, to reduce one's denominator, as Thoreau advised—these might be the means of survival in the contemporary Waste Land.

In "Slobs of the Kitchen Sea," one of the sketches in *Lonesome Traveler* about his life in the early forties, Jack escapes from New York aboard a ship. He says, "I pictured myself with grave face pointed seaward through the final Gate of Golden America never to return. . . ." He will not dwell on "the dark farcical furious real life of this roaring working world" (pp. 89–90). In *Vanity of Duluoz*, after marrying "Johnny" (Edie Parker) and having been put in jail as an accessory to the supposed murder of Franz Mueller (actually a suicide), Jack listens to the prisoners' snores in the middle of the night and thinks of the Chinese brothers in prison. He thinks of the rice in their father's shop, the ink under his father's fingernails, and his own position. It all seems ridiculous that men should work so hard only to be going nowhere. Then he thinks, "Absurdity? Of course there's someplace to go! Go mind your own business" (p. 254). In this period, 1944–1945, when, as he says, he joined the "despairists," we find Kerouac and his heroes giving up on the world and ready for the isolation that later becomes a withdrawal in pursuit of Godhead.

Early in his travels in *Big Sur*, where he oscillates between the wilds of the Monterey coast and the sociable wildness of San Francisco, Jack tells himself to quietly watch the world, to ask no longer why God is torturing him, ". . . to be a loner, travel, talk to waiters only . . . it's time to think and watch and keep concentrated on the fact that . . . the world as we know it now will be covered with the silt of a billion years in time. . . . Yay, for this, more aloneness . . ." (p. 24). The aloneness brings revelation and the possibility of concentration on man's insignificance, reducing the denominator, reducing desire, slowing time's "vicious change."

But aloneness can never last for long, no matter how much peace it brings, and often it brings nightmares instead of peace. Climbing a mountain with Japhy Ryder in *Dharma Bums*, Ray Smith crouches on a ledge waiting for the more intrepid Japhy to come down from the summit. He fears the "impossible horrors" of "huge mountains and rock and empty space," yet he also has the continual feeling that he has been here before, sometime in the ancestral past (p. 67). Like the image of the dark Merrimac, the mountain is a symbol of primordial time out of which somehow, blindly, absurdly life has sprung. Life cannot melt back into the rock. It is alienated so long as it is living, enduring its estranged condition until death. In *Big Sur* Jack looks at the primordial landscape and a mountain that reminds him of a mountain in a dream that has been haunting him, the mountain of Mien Mo, a thousand miles high, once the home of the gods but now with its giant stone benches vacated and cobwebbed, and himself in the dream crawling through narrow dusty holes with tomato plants tied around his neck, groveling and lost (pp. 16–17). There are no gods to make sense of man's separation from inert matter. In his aloneness his spiritual hunger becomes an incubus from which there seems to be no escape.

Kerouac's earliest extensive encounter with nature alone occurred when he served as a fire lookout for approximately eight weeks on Desolation Peak in the Cascade Mountains in the summer of 1956. The reactions to that adventure were first written out in an article, "Alone on a Mountaintop," and later made into the first chapter of *Desolation Angels*. His reactions to solitude, contemplation of nature, and the enforced withdrawal into his own mind are complete in this one experience.

Upon first arriving at his lookout, his reaction is quite

positive. It seems to be an ideal place for contemplation. As he looks out at the fog-shrouded mountain scene around him, he imagines a Chinese, like Hanshan, writing poems on cliffs similar to the ones he sees and meditating on the meaning or meaninglessness of the void, of illusion and reality. For a time the actions of the mice in the cupboard, the wild flowers outside, and the terrifying drama of a mountain thunderstorm occupy his attention. Then listening to his shortwave radio and the comments of other lookouts breaks the loneliness somewhat, but gradually the solitude becomes overpowering. On Sundays "the sun is too golden bright." Sunday, he says, is "God's lookingglass," but he is not ready for the Golden Eternity (p. 31). As Eliot says in *Four Quartets*, "The mind cannot bear too much reality." The bright emergence of mystic oneness that the solitary mystic seeks is, when encountered in a corresponding natural state (radiant sunlight in clear mountain air), too much for mortal flesh and mortal mind to bear. And near the end of his two-month stay he has had so much of inward contemplation that he has reached the bottom of the self and found there "abysmal nothingness worst [sic] than that no illusion even—my mind's in rags" (p. 61).

Coming down from the mountain is a relief from feeding on his empty self, and once down he also realizes "the vision of the freedom of eternity which I saw and which all wilderness hermitage saints have seen, is of little use in cities and warring societies such as we have" (p. 66). Back in civilization, though, he feels keenly the loss of tranquility and saintliness, as he says, "I cant for the life of me be anything but enraged, lost, partial, critical, mixed-up, scared, foolish, proud, sneering, shit shit shit—" (p. 71). Like Eliot's Edward and Livinia in his play *The Cocktail Party*, Jack finds that living nobly and lovingly in the world of men is at least as difficult as the escape into mystic contemplation and entails making "the best of a bad job."

Looking at a caterpillar, one of the few bits of life about him on the mountain, Jack sees him "upsidedown and clinging to his sphere" and remarks, "We are all mad." He goes on to think of his travels down the coast as possibly just as "sad and mad," but then thinks, "bejesus j Christ it'll be bettern hangin around *this* rock." If the world is absurd, if the meaning is unknowable, we still feel a compulsion to move, to experience, to act. In Kerouac's own poetic words, "We live to long, so long I will, and jounce down that mountain highest perfect knowing or no highest perfect knowing full of glorious ignorant looking to sparkle elsewhere—" (pp. 32–33). The experience is similar at Big Sur when he tries to write poetry while listening to the sounds of the sea. Jack concludes that the sea is like God; it does not want us there recording it. He has had enough of communion with meaningless nature and decides to go to his "desire." He quits Big Sur for San Francisco (*Big Sur*, pp. 41–42).

The whole adventure in San Francisco and Big Sur is full of *angst*, and it climaxes in what the existential philosopher Kierkegaard calls the "sickness unto death." Waking up with delirium tremens, Duluoz describes it as the "final horrors." He describes it as feeling "a guilt so deep you identify yourself with the devil and God seems far away abandoning you to your sick silliness—You feel sick in the greatest sense of the word, breathing without believing in it . . ." (*Big Sur*, p. 111). Later, with Billie, he says he is afraid and wants to go home to die with his cat. Like Gerard, with whom his cats are always identified, Jack wants to escape to Heaven. The shambles of his dream of heroism, of what the American success myth had led him to expect as a child, surrounds him, *is* him, when he says, "I could be a handsome thin young president, in a suit sitting in an old fashioned rocking chair, no instead I'm just the Phantom of the Opera standing by a drape among dead fish and broken chairs—Can it be that no one cares who made me or why?" (p. 168). The vigorous, youthful president, rich and seemingly at ease in his rocking chair (ironically, Jack Kennedy used the rocking chair to ease chronic back pain dating back to a war injury), is the very picture of the success-

ful young man that Memère had prayed her son would become. In accepting lostness "forever" in 1944, he cut himself
off from the normal societal paths to success, in hopes of a
brighter illumination that would sanctify his difference and
bring him a sense of completion and joy. The quest after
ecstasy has failed to bring him the fruits he has sought, and his
success as an artist has brought him little positive recognition
from the public at large. He looks back sick with regret.

Later, at Big Sur, once again having the d.t.'s, the water
in the stream tastes like gasoline, and the shrubbery seems to
be reaching out to strangle him. Dave Wain (Lew Welch)
comes to the stream to clean a freshly caught fish and speaks
of the fish as a sacrificial meal for a new beginning for Duluoz
and his Beat friends. And after tortured dreams in which there
is a vision of the cross and a symbolic burial of the past, he
falls into a refreshing sleep, awaking once again with hope as
the sickness fades away and his *angst* is relieved. His native
energies reassert themselves, and from his most wretched in-
wardness he begins again to reach out toward life. The cycle
recommences.

The perpetual withdrawal from and return to active life
parallels the earlier cyclical escapes onto the road away from
society and family. Duluoz and Cody and their counterparts
in all the novels are unable to stay with any human relationship long enough to experience its day-to-day growth over a
long period of time. Their view of life is, therefore, frag-
mented. They do not see it as an ongoing process that has its
own logic of growth. D. L. Stevenson in his article on James
Jones and Jack Kerouac has noted that the characters' lives are
always shown in "cut-off fragments of time." The events of
the novels seem "mutually exclusive and have no communi-
cative fictive significance." Speaking of *On the Road*, he says,
"We know nothing cumulative or coherent about Sal Paradise
or Dean Moriarty at all."[8] What continuity we do have in the
characters' lives comes from viewing the Duluoz Legend as a
whole, and the fact remains that the events seem repetitious

and without dependence upon one another. The lack of any consequential series of events and the lack of character growth has caused one critic, Melvin Askew, to remark that in *On the Road* "there are hundreds of episodes and actions, but not one experience."[9] The values of the society are so readily rejected by the characters that lives lived and developed according to those values are apparently thought not worth the author's or his heroes' close observation or analysis. The quest for ecstasy, chiliastic or Buddhistic, has as its by-product the loss of continuity in living time.

When ecstasy fails, there is no sense of ongoing life to fall back upon. Kerouac's attempts to establish a sense of continuity, though, show his deep desire to return to the main current of historical time. The very same Merrimac that he sees as a raging evil force is also a symbol of continuing primal history. The Merrimac created "dark valleys," and in one of them Lowell developed, with its "great trees of antiquity . . . waving over lost arrowheads . . . , the pebbles on the slatecliff beach are full of hidden beads and were stepped on barefoot by Indians" (*Sax*, p. 8). He is very proud of his lineage, too, and made an effort while in Europe to establish contact with his Breton relatives. In *Vanity of Duluoz* the ancient lineage is used as a rationalization for his being "well nigh sterile" (p. 257). In his later years he felt frequent regret that he had no one except Memère to share his life with and that he was probably going to die without heirs. It was some comfort to think that he was one of the last of a line of aristocrats, decadent in a decadent age. With him time would "have a stop" for the Kerouacs (Duluozes); the best lives had already been lived.

In *Nothing More to Declare* John Clellon Holmes says Kerouac thought of Beatness as "a weariness with all the forms, all the conventions of the world."[11] Further on, Holmes says, "In short, it means being undramatically pushed up against the wall of oneself. A man is beat whenever he goes for broke and wagers the sum of his resources on a single number . . ." (p. 110). Kerouac's heroes are quintessentially Beat in all these respects. With the loss of family and community and the dark knowledge of the rapacious life in the more fluid society beyond, the hero quests aimlessly for his lost union of family and friends. He learns that no one really cares sufficiently for others outside the family or established community and tries to accept the loss of *caritas*. The evil of a society that simply does not care enough is too painful, however, and there is naturally a strong resentment against social pressures to conform to the loveless social standards of money-grubbing and material accumulation. Unable to find love in perfect union in society, the hero tries to find it in ecstatic union with the Universe and God. He is, indeed, wagering "the sum of his resources on a single number."

His quest for oneness, for perfect love and harmony, begins as a time-annihilating burst of speed with Dean Moriarty at the wheel, then moves to an isolated contemplation of nature, which leaves the mind "in rags." Nature's movements appear insane. Man controlled by natural drives for self-aggrandizement makes a mockery of man's attempts to lead a morally good and ordered existence. Man's appetite for personal gain is too great for him to successfully deny himself, and his vision too short-sighted to keep his desiring from hurting him. His only safety from himself will come with his death.

His gamble on ecstasy and his attempts at self-denial ending in failure, the hero thinks regretfully how it might have been if he had been able to live by the illusions of the larger society and successfully to conform to the demands of the workaday world of business and family. He is painfully aware that he has made no real attempts to merge himself once again with an established community and that he has continually refused the responsibility of developing his own family. What seemed at the time a proper rejection in favor of individual freedom and purpose had come to mean to Kerouac in the 1960s a condemnation to everlasting loneliness.

5

The Golden Eternity

IN *THE DHARMA BUMS* Ray Smith says that society was probably best avoided altogether and he was not interested in Alvah's (Ginsberg's) "ideas about grasping after life as much as you can because of its sweet sadness and because you would be dead some day" (p. 84). After his time-blurring experiences with Cody, the author-hero, now a student of Buddhism, feels that what he wants to do is to do nothing, merely to "rest and be kind" (p. 84). He is ready to practice a Taoist quietism that will bring him back into the primal stream of time, in consonance with nature and growing things, feeling only the most basic sensations, in what Henry Miller calls "the state of the happy rock," or what Walt Whitman says is an imperturbable state in which one confronts life as "the trees and the animals do." The difficulty for Kerouac, as with Miller and Whitman, is simply that Western civilized man is not so easily reducible to this condition. The urge to action and creation and the social desire for recognition are not so easily submerged into a vegetative existence. His attempt to reduce time to manageable dimensions is doomed to failure, although in his withdrawals from human society, recorded in *Dharma Bums, Desolation Angels*, and *Big Sur*, he tries again and again.

One of William Blake's Proverbs of Hell is: "If the doors of perception were cleansed every thing would appear to man as it is, infinite." Kerouac's quest for the infinite led him to Buddhism as a means of cleansing his perception. He began seriously reading Buddhist texts in January 1954, and the next year he was writing a biography of Buddha called "Wake Up" (unpublished), and a book of "translations" tentatively titled "Some of the Dharma" or "What the Buddha Tells Us" (also unpublished).[1] His published work from *Dharma Bums* onward is heavily imbued with Buddhist thought, as he and his characters try to reduce the threat of the destructive world around them.

In the 22nd Chorus of *Mexico City Blues* Kerouac says that he was an "importunate fool" who "raved to fight Saviors" rather than quietly listen, "still a fool," but in his acceptance of his own insignificance and ignorance, finally, a wise fool. He has sought the "do nothing" state of mind that the Chinese call *Wu Wei*, "a kind of cloistral fervor in the midst of mad ranting action-seekers of this or any other 'modern' world" (*Desolation*, pp. 219–220).

The modern world that he rejects is maya (an illusion), and a mad one at that. The Beats are continually reminding themselves that the ways of the world are nonsense. It is symbolic that the characters in *Pull My Daisy* (1959) exit to a chorus of "Da, da, da, da . . . ," a throw-back to Tristan Tzara and the Dadaist nonsense revolt against the ways of society after World War I. When Jack leaves the little Japanese Zen master, George, at the hospital in *Big Sur*, they play a gradually distancing game of hide and seek, showing gradually less and less of themselves, until, as a final gesture, George throws a glass of water out of the hospital window, symbolically a final vaporizing loss of form in a world that takes the forms of things too seriously (pp. 82–83). When Jack and Arthur Ma, the Chinese Zen-ist, engage in a drunken, stichometric, Dadaist dialog on the beach at Big Sur, it is also to remind themselves not to take philosophy and religion, and indeed any system of abstract thought, too seriously (p. 101). That human

thought can give order to the world is in Buddhist terms also
an illusion.

Real satori (enlightenment) comes not through rational
thought but through intuition, mystical insight. Much of the
novice's training in Buddhism is devoted to disrupting his
usual, logical patterns of response, making him see, feel, or
imagine without conscious, verbal thought. Satori is an intense,
emotional release resulting in an ecstatic awareness of unity
and wholeness. It is not an analytical procedure. Rational
thought only vitiates the emotional content of perception and
falsifies its nature. Concepts take us beyond the felt reality.
To know the true meaning of our perceptions, the Buddhist
would have us not escape into thought, but dwell with our felt
responses, accepting them, becoming intensely aware of them
until the central trend of feeling (the Tao) emerges.

In *Dharma Bums* Ray Smith (Kerouac) says that he has
told Japhy Ryder that he does not care much about the mythology of Buddhism but is interested in the first of the "Four
Noble Truths": All life is suffering. He was also interested in
the fourth truth, which he did not yet quite believe: The sup-
pression of suffering can be achieved. He goes on to say that
after digesting the Lankavatra Sutra he could see that the
fourth truth was possible since there is nothing in the world
but mind, and if the mind can interpret what it sees as other
than suffering, then suffering can be suppressed (p. 12). The
difficulty, however, is in the reinterpretation. Japhy throws a
stick at Smith's foot, and although Smith feels it, he continues
to deny the reality of the sensation. (Dr. Johnson kicked a
stone to disprove Bishop Berkeley's solipsistic idealism. Perhaps the bishop would have responded the same way if Johnson had thrown the stone at him!) Earlier in their relationship
Smith tells Japhy just how great he feels hiking, and Japhy
responds by saying, "it's all the same old void, boy" (p. 45).
And although intellectually they agree that the world is illusion and beyond it is nothing but the void, Smith's sensation
of good feeling is very real to him no matter what the Buddhist

says. Calling physical happenings illusions does not change the way they are sensed.

Kerouac interprets the Buddhist attitude toward the illusions of our senses as follows: first, because they are factitious they are essentially meaningless; second, because they are meaningless there is no point in labeling them good or evil; third, because the world has no true reality and there is no good or evil, there is nothing for us to do in it except to exist, to accept the wonder of the illusion, to be kind to all who are afflicted by it, and to know that death marks the end of it and a return to the perfect void. The concept of the blissful void is comforting to the nihilist, for if all we normally perceive and think is maya and undecipherable nonsense, then he is relieved of the necessity of trying to make sense of the world and relieved of blame when things go wrong in it. Yet, at the same time it is most disturbing, because we do, after all, "live to be fooled" and for some reason "fool to be alive" (*Desolation*, p. 51). He looks for a necessary connection between the world and the void, but when he yells across Desolation Mountain, "What is the meaning of the void?" he is answered with perfect silence (*Traveler*, p. 128). The void has no meaning in worldly terms. We know of its existence only by knowing its opposite, maya, the illusionary world of objects. As Rol Sturlason says in *Dharma Bums*, discussing with Ray Smith the design of a monastery garden, "It's only through form that we can realize emptiness" (p. 21).

The universe is a cosmic play that takes many opposing forms, and like Milarepa we are to believe: "The more Ups and Downs the more Joy I feel—The greater the fear, the greater the happiness I feel . . ." (*Big Sur*, p. 121). In short, we are to synchronize ourselves with the opposing forces of the universe and in so doing partake will-lessly of the wondrous expression of the power that we find in the myriad forms of maya. "The Power delights in all of it—It is reminding itself that it is the Power, that's why, for it, The Power, is really only ecstasy, and its manifestations dream, it is the Golden

Eternity, ever peaceful . . ." (*Desolation*, p. 28). When lightning flashes during a storm while Jack is in his lookout on the
mountain, he thinks, "It really is dreadful, but the passer-
through-everything must really feel good about everything that
happens, the lucky exuberant bastard—(cancer's exuberant)—
so if a lightning bolt disintegrates Jack Duluoz in his Desolation, smile . . ." (p. 39).

In *Visions of Gerard* the author says that death is the "only
decent subject, since it marks the end of illusion and delusion."
Also, since the world is imaginary, not real, we should do
"nothing—nothing—nothing," only be kind and patient and
"fine" (p. 123). In the 33rd Chorus of *Mexico City Blues* he
speaks of William Burroughs and probably of himself when
he says, "I'm an idealist/ who has outgrown/ my idealism/ I
have nothing to do/ the rest of my life/ but do it/ and the rest
of my life/ to do it" (p. 33). He has given up any thought of
reform in human nature and will act in the world as the Tao
is revealed to him.

On Desolation Mountain, Jack awaits the coming of Ava-
lokitesvara, the famous cloud-horse of Buddhist mythology, who
carries those who are ready to nirvana (a state of extinguished
desire). This Buddhist savior never comes for Jack, for he cannot attain his state, that of one who is "aware of the light
material the world is made of, yet . . . never discoursed, nor
communicated by signs, nor wasted a breath complaining"
(*Traveler*, p. 131). Jack is unable to attain the degree of tolerance for the world as it is that is required.

Some of Kerouac's critics have accused him of not being
faithful to Zen doctrines. Ironically, Kerouac's primary alle-
giance was not to Zen at all but to Mahayana Buddhism. Zen
compromises with active, worldly existence, and, as such, condemns man to exist in a world of temptation and evil (*Desolation*, p. 267). The Mahayana Buddhist sees all men moving
toward Buddhahood, a heavenly state of wise kindness and
quiescent acceptance. This state is the final escape from the
temptation-impelled cycles of karma (fate), a final end to end-

less rebirth and struggle. For Kerouac, "The essential teaching of the Lord Buddha was: 'No More Rebirth' . . ." (p. 267). Elsewhere, Kerouac says that the quest for nirvana (to get out of the cycle of rebirth) is "ultimately silly," since the dead are not reborn in this world anyway. They are, instead, a part of the silent, peaceful void (*Traveler*, p. 132).

Void or world, Kerouac comforts himself and his dharma bums with the thought that everything and nothing are all part of the Golden Eternity. In the *Scripture of the Golden Eternity* he says that we are here because we are a part of the Golden Eternity, and that being so we cannot help but be pure, for man naturally desires the good.[2] Nevertheless, he admits, in this life we are at the mercy of our karma, by which he no doubt means our limited perception, the temptations of the flesh, and the forces of the universe. Because we are essentially pure beings, however, we are already saved, already a part of God, Buddha, the Golden Eternity (or whatever one might wish to call it). As Gerard says after dreaming of the Virgin Mary, . . . we're all in Heaven—but we dont know it!" (*Gerard*, p. 68).

We would do well, then, to adopt the role of Alf, the Sacred Burro in *Big Sur* that waits patiently in the corral for someone to give him an apple. He is sacred in his patient acceptance of things and for bearing biblically what was more defenseless and greater than he. Our foolish questionings will avail us naught. What is required is patience, fortitude, and faith.

The sense of mystery in life is strong in Kerouac. In *Visions of Gerard* he says, "That there *is* a world, that, rather, there *seems* to be a world, is hugely more interesting than what tiddly diddly well might happen in it . . ." (pp. 122–123). He is continually finding evidence of divinity in our illusory existence. On Desolation Mountain he speaks of going outside for a walk and finding his shadow ringed by a rainbow as he walks on the hilltop. It seems to him "a lovely haloed mystery," and it makes him want to pray. As he moves on, however, the desolation becomes more overpowering as he notes, "A blade of grass jiggling in the winds of infinity, anchored to a rock, and for your own poor gentle flesh no answer." He concludes that the human mind is an "oil lamp burning in infinity" (*Traveler*, p. 130). Hiking in the Sierras with Japhy Ryder, he speaks of hearing the roar of silence in the purple dusk of sunset, "a wash of diamond waves going through the liquid porches of our ears, enough to soothe a man a thousand years" (*Dharma Bums*, p. 57). Although the experience is completely happy, he also sees it as completely hallucinated. Mystic indications of divine mystery are no sooner received than doubted because the indications are, after all, known through the senses or the mind and both are purveyors of maya. To a great extent, then, it is, peculiarly enough, Kerouac's Buddhism that frustrates his desire to know God through mystical experience.

In the late sixties Kerouac claimed that he was really an old-fashioned Catholic mystic. Maya was not such an impediment to knowing the One in Catholicism. The physical world was supposed to be full of evidences of His existence, and a believer did not have to have complete satori to have communion with Him.

As early as 1959 he was responding to his critics who accused him of being nihilistic with statements of affirmation. In an article in *Playboy* that year he says that he wants "to speak for things" and he goes on to ask us to not just live our lives but to "*love*" them out. "Who knows, my God," he asks, "but that this universe is not one vast sea of compassion actually, the veritable holy honey, beneath all this show of personality and cruelty . . . ?"[33] In *Visions of Gerard*, written three years earlier, he had said, "I see no reason for Man—But his value, I buy" (p. 116). In *Dharma Bums* it is Smith (Kerouac) who says he does not believe in reincarnation or hell but that all souls "go straight to nirvana Heaven." He also tells Japhy Ryder that he loves Christ and says it is because Christ preached love that He is important (p. 159). In 1960 Kerouac wrote in the preface to *Lonesome Traveler* that his chief complaint about the contemporary world was the "facetiousness of 'respectable' people . . . who, because not taking anything seriously, are destroying old human feelings older than *Time Magazine*" (p. vi). In the final analysis Kerouac wanted very much to believe in a beneficent God at the heart of things and in the value of human life. His fear-ridden hopes for man's earthly future are concisely expressed in a letter to Ginsberg, 28 October 1958, in which he says he does not agree "Bomb world-apocalypse is good, I believe in people saying it won't happen at all because we evolve now and become smart human race. I hope."[4]

In Kerouac's work the key to love is complete acceptance of everything as Divine, "For when you realize that God is Everything you know that you've got to love everything no matter how bad it is . . . ." Things are really neither good nor bad but just simply *are*, or what is "made to appear." He sees our phenomenal world as "some kind of drama to teach something to something, some 'despiséd substance of divinest show' " (*Traveler*, p. 132).

The key to acceptance is to "form no preconceptions whatever in your mind" (*Traveler*, p. 132). But here we have a grave difficulty. It is all but impossible to function in the world without preconceptions (values, judgments, beliefs) of one sort or another. Refusal to evaluate and discriminate may not be necessary for one in a mystical trance, going back to that time "when your eyes were bright/ with seeing emptiness/ in the void of holy sea/ where creatures didn't/ abound, nor crops grow,/ and nothing happened,/ and nobody lived/ and nobody cared—."[5] But in the phenomenal world in which we have our human existence the apprehension of its reality and its laws of behavior depend upon the exercise of just those powers of reason that the romantic disparages.

Alan Watts, one of the foremost popularizers of Zen Buddhism in America, has noted that it is a "basic intuition" of Zen "that there is an ultimate standpoint from which 'anything goes' " and that distinctions disappear "when human affairs are seen as part and parcel of the whole realm of nature." Nevertheless, "within the conventional limits of human community there are clear distinctions between good and evil."[6] Just as Kerouac preferred the more mystical Mahayana Buddhism to Zen because he wished to de-emphasize the cycle of earthly existence and concentrate on a union with Godhead, so he tends to ignore the "conventional limits of human community" and to blur distinctions of good and evil by viewing human life from the "ultimate standpoint." His recipe for human relations in #52 of *The Scripture of the Golden Eternity* expresses his view very well: "By practicing kindness all over with everyone you will soon come into the holy trance, definite distinctions of personalities will become what they really mysteriously are . . . even and one thing everywhere the holy eternal milky love, . . . the compassion in the sound of silence . . ." (p. 39). It is indeed doubtful that one can successfully deal with individual human beings, their fears and desires, hates and affections by treating each one as something so amorphous as "eternal milky love," "holy" or not.

As pointed out in the previous chapter, the quest for ecstasy on the part of the Kerouac heroes overshadows ideals of human responsibility and love. The quest for Godhead reduces individual human beings to personae acting in a movie of the mind. The script is their karma, and their only value is as momentary emanations of the *jeu d'esprit* of the Director Eternal. Their loves and hates, their successes and their sufferings are all ephemeral masks of "the same old void," having no meaning in themselves and therefore not to be taken very seriously. The Buddhist way of coping with suffering is to deny it, and although Kerouac knew that total denial of what our senses tell us is impossible in this life, he could gain some ascendancy over the pain by noting its cosmic insignificance. He could also compensate for man's worldly ignorance and failure of *caritas* by suggesting that worldly love and knowledge are also insignificant in cosmic terms. In *Desolation*

Angels he says that the only true or good thing he ever heard was Buddha adjuring us to be mindful of eternity. Although such awareness will not do us any *earthly* good, Buddha asks us to be "Great Knowers Without Knowing, Great Lovers Beyond Love" (p. 20), so that our concepts of knowledge and love go beyond earthly life to the desired union with Godhead.

When Kerouac's persona attains the highest perfect wisdom (111th Chorus of *Mexico City Blues*), he attains "absolutely nothing" and abides in "blank ecstasy." Scripture #64 in *Scripture of the Golden Eternity* suggests that Kerouac did indeed have, at least once, an experience that he considered a true satori; and since the knowledge which he sought is the knowledge that there is no knowledge and that the void alone exists eternally, the highest wisdom attained would be, for him and the Buddhist mystic, "absolutely nothing." (The "blank ecstasy" of revelation is common to descriptions of mystical experience in the writings of both Eastern and Western mystics from the author of the Diamond Sutra to St. John of the Cross.)

Kerouac's venture into Buddhism enabled him to dissolve the complex forms of day-to-day living into nothingness. By refusing to establish a balance between uncontrollable forces of life on the one hand and death on the other, he shifts from one absurd view to another. On the one hand the world is too complex and too uncontrollable to be fully understood or fully ordered, and on the other hand there is simply nothing to bother ordering. The relative existence that most men are willing to accept as sufficiently real and substantial for them to work and achieve in is not one that Kerouac will accept. It is all or nothing, and at the end of the Buddhist road all and nothing are the same thing. He has made a quick circle from childish visions of perfect love and peace through the distasteful world of experience to a somewhat more refined view of the child's innocent vision.

It is probably to Kerouac's credit as a novelist that he had sufficient concern with human suffering and expressions of human vitality to find denial of suffering truly impossible and extended isolation and meditation boring. As Ann Charters makes clear in her biography, he died not in peaceful meditation but in a state of terrible loneliness, unable to deny the need for human love and appreciation which a complete escape into mysticism might have negated. Because his suffering is that of his characters, and because both represent the agony of existential twentieth-century man, for whom man's destiny and reason for being are all but impossible to fathom, Kerouac's vision of the Golden Eternity is, in the last analysis, the final measurement of his despair.

6

Spontaneous Prose

JOHN CLELLON HOLMES, who read the manuscripts of *The Town and the City* and *On the Road* before they were published, met Kerouac in New York in the summer of 1948. In his memoir of the late forties and early fifties, *Nothing More to Declare*, Holmes says that what he got from talking to Kerouac and reading his material was "not a voice, but an eye." Kerouac advised him that "reality is details" and that he should "cut as close to the bone of the detail as words would go," that "punctuation was the movie-music of prose," and that "form should be poetically satisfying, rather than mechanically demonstrable." In the end the writer's book should be one that he himself would "most want to read," and to be successful, a writer had to "amass a daily heap of words." Also according to Holmes, Kerouac advocated that the author cultivate a careful detachment, to preserve his prose from becoming pretentious or sentimental (p. 75).

Before *On the Road* was published in 1957, Kerouac was moving away from these precepts and was experimenting with what he called Spontaneous Prose. In May 1951 he wrote a considerable amount of *On the Road* on a hundred-foot roll of paper using dashes for punctuation. He later had to revise what he had written several times and ended up allowing the publisher to punctuate it in the standard way.[1] He had written

Town and the City according to what he was taught about writing at Columbia, but later he felt that the book was dead.[2] He started *On the Road* in the same fashion, and it is the early work on that book that Holmes speaks of in *Nothing More to Declare*. The precepts Holmes gives us sound like extracts from Hemingway's *Death in the Afternoon* or the pronouncements of one of Kerouac's Columbia professors who was taken with Ezra Pound's and Ernest Hemingway's contributions to the theory of writing. It is particularly ironic that Kerouac's adjuration to avoid pretentiousness and sentimentality was one he could never successfully follow. His critics never failed to fault him on both counts in all of his fiction.

Kerouac claimed that he decided to become a writer at seventeen. He was inspired to do so by young Sebastian Sampas, brother of Kerouac's third wife. Sampas was one of the neighborhood gang in Lowell and an aspiring young poet. Kerouac later called him his Verlaine. Sampas was killed at Anzio in World War II. Kerouac spent part of the war years at sea in the merchant marine and hitchhiking across the country, emulating the life of Jack London. Other influences in those early years were Saroyan, Hemingway, and Wolfe.[3] By far the most influential were the latter two.

The Town and the City is the earliest and most Wolfean novel. In a review of the book in *Newsweek* Kerouac is compared to Wolfe and Sinclair Lewis. Kerouac is said to have Lewis's keen eye for externals without Lewis's sarcasm or mockery. He is praised for infusing grandeur into the simple doings of daily life, like Wolfe, although he tends to overwrite, and "the long-winded nonsense of his intellectuals is well-nigh unreadable."[4] V. P. Haas's review in the Chicago *Sun-Tribune* praises Kerouac for his "clarity, compassion, and force," but faults him for his "flood of rhetoric which dissipates the unquestioned power of the novel in useless incident and endless conversation which contributes nothing to the building of character through action."[5] By his sticking closely to the Wolfean style, Wolfe's weaknesses as well as his strengths became Kerouac's as well.

Even after he began to write more spontaneously and the influences of his reading the sutras and the work of Henry Miller became larger in his work, Kerouac retained a basic perspective on his material that is akin to that of Wolfe. He says in *Visions of Cody*, ". . . my own complete life, an endless contemplation, is so interesting, I love it so, it is vast, goes everywhere" (p. 98). The interest is in forms, surface brilliancies, and in visions of childhood that largely govern the man. Also, like Wolfe, he endeavors to seize experience whole and to hold it thus, stopping time.[6]

The attempt to record all of the experience, to get it all in, reaches a questionable stage in part three, "Frisco: The Tape," of *Visions of Cody*. This section is a literal transcription of the taped conversations between Jack and Neal and Neal's wife, Carolyn, and a few other people. At such a point in his work, one wonders if the author has not wholly lost his art in his material; but as Ginsberg points out in the introduction to the book, the "Tape" may have relation to the sort of thing that Andy Warhol did with the Campbell Soup cans. It may be a way of denying the validity of an author's impressing form upon his subject matter. Instead, the form is made to emerge on its own from the material, sliced in this case from real conversation. The author's only function here is to focus our senses on a narrow transcription of experience isolated from the ruck of his and our other, irrelevant impressions, enabling us to see, perhaps for the first time, just what the rhythms of thought and speech are in minds plagued by the anxieties of our time.

Nevertheless, the author's attempt to "get it all in" has caused his critics to lament his lack of discrimination. Peter Sourian, speaking of Kerouac's last novel, *Vanity of Duluoz*, accuses him of "assuming that what has happened to him is automatically valuable."[7] As early as the publication of *Maggie Cassidy*, one of his critics, John Ciardi, was to say, "The total premise of such writing seems to be: 'Oh, my God it happened to *me*: every sacred, formless irrelevance is out of my own loving memory of myself."[8] To the translator of Dante such narcissism is unpardonable. But like Blake, Whitman, and Wolfe, Kerouac started always from the self as the center of his being and the surest source of what he knew. That, unlike either of his progenitors, he never expanded his work into complex religious myth or a vision of America's becoming may say more about the cynical thrust of the age than it does about Kerouac's obvious immaturity.

Seymour Krim says that Kerouac has actually let "some of the real experience of our decade escape into his pages in crude, free-swinging, even shapeless form." Further on, Krim says, "What sets Kerouac apart from the 'writer writers' and makes his voice carry, despite its comparative frailty and childishness, is that he has the courage to put down the unaccustomed rhythm and details of the frantic modern scene exactly the way he's lived it." *The Subterraneans* he finds a particularly vivid piece of writing that "stays in the mind like a burr."[9]

Wolfe had, of course, captured the sensations of the moment in memorable scenes in his novels, such as the scene of the fire in the Jacks' apartment building in New York (in *You Can't Go Home Again*) or the chapter on the Oktoberfest (in *The Web and the Rock*). Kerouac, however, was trying to go him one better. He was seeking to express the intensity of the moment and to capture the rush of sensations in a prose in which the sense impressions tumble in, one on top of the other, building a sense of movement and anxiety which is the very antithesis of form and order but which Kerouac must have felt was truer to the pace and unresolvable tangle of modern life.

In *Desolation Angels* Kerouac tells us that after being discharged from the navy as a schizoid personality, because he could not take discipline, he became an ambitious paranoid, writing to justify his belief in life. He says that these "earnest scribblings . . . were the first of their kind in the world." He wrote them, he claims, without hope of having them published.

These pieces were the beginnings of what he later called Spontaneous Prose (p. 229).

The first novel to illustrate his new prose was *On the Road*. Ann Charters has suggested that the rushing prose of this work was influenced by William Burroughs's "factual" style in *Junkie* and the rapid, roaring prose of one of Neal Cassady's letters, both of which Kerouac read in 1951 before he typed out his hundred-foot roll of *On the Road* prose. In writing *Junkie* Burroughs put his descriptive and lecturelike material together without much concern for chronology or overall coherence. Cassady's letter was written while he was high on benzedrine. It was a forty-page, single-spaced missive about his love affair with one Joan Anderson, and its heightened color and rush of images captivated Kerouac. Ginsberg says that the letter was the paramount influence on Kerouac's adopting a spontaneous style.[10]

In his book on the Beats, Bruce Cook also notes the influence of jazz on Kerouac's style. And it is certainly true that in his own pronouncements on the subject of writing Kerouac inevitably uses the vocabulary of jazz to illustrate what he is trying to do:

> Not selectivity of expression but following free deviation (association) of mind into limitless blow-on-subject seas of thought, swimming in sea of English with no discipline other than rhythms of rhetorical exhalation and expostulated statement, like a fist coming down on a table with each complete utterance, bang! (the space dash)—Blow as deep as you want—write as deeply, fish as far down as you want, satisfy yourself first, then reader cannot fail to receive telepathic shock and meaning-excitement by same laws operating in his own human mind.[11]

Aside from the improvisation of jazz, the method he prescribes also related to the efforts of various poets to speak their feelings without regard for set modes of expression. The development of a prose rhythm from exhalation and gesture is similar to the idea of the contemporary poet Charles Olson that the length of the poetic line should be determined by the breath of the poet. The idea that by digging far down into the self and letting the pent-up stream of feelings come forth un-impeded, finding their own form in words, the author is re-leasing ideas of superior purity and significance is an age-old romantic belief. Blake claimed he wrote *Milton* responding without effort to a voice within him. Yeats claimed he wrote in trances. André Breton and the Surrealists sought to tap the well of the subconscious directly through automatic writing and free association. Kerouac told Cook that he wrote with the Holy Ghost speaking through him (p. 90).

The faster and more effortless the writing, the more true it would be, or so these authors seemed to believe. To this end Kerouac suggests that the author should set up a definite image or object before his mind and then "blow" directly from the mind on the subject of the image. To avoid the artificial pauses of conventional punctuation, he recommends using only "the vigorous space dash," which represents, in the words of William Carlos Williams, "measured pauses which are the essentials of our speech."[12] Williams had already shown in *Paterson* that punctuation could be cut down a great deal and had instituted the dash for similar purposes. The Black Mountain poets Charles Olson, Robert Duncan, and Robert Creeley used the Objectivist theories of Williams and gave them a certain cur-rency among the poets of the fifties. Kerouac was obviously making use of some of their ideas in the formulation of prin-ciples for Spontaneous Prose.

In their poetry, however, the Black Mountain poets are not nearly so formless as Kerouac. Both Duncan and Creeley, par-ticularly, are poets of tight compression and relatively unified imagery. Kerouac's poetry has been universally damned by his reviewers because of its sloppiness and vacuity. The best of it is probably contained in *Mexico City Blues*. Much of it is echolalic verbiage that sounds like a horn player trying the scale while tuning up. The powerful image at the center of the poem, a cardinal necessity in Williams's poetics, is most often simply not there. The subject matter is nearly always connected with the idea that life is an illusion and therefore not worth fretting about.

The 28th Chorus of *Mexico City Blues* amply illustrates what is wrong with Kerouac's poetry:

> —And you seek to achieve
> Greater satisfaction
> Which is already impossible
> Because of Supreme Reality and Time
> And Timelessness Entire
> All conjoined & arranged & finished
> By Karmas of Rue
> In heavenlands remote—
> You suffer & you fall,
> You discriminate a ball.

The first six lines of this passage are an abstract philosophical statement. The last four contain an image which is a play on words, "Karmas of Rue," and the metaphor for a self-contained, closed system, "a ball." The metaphoric density, the intensity of imagery, in the poem is slight indeed. The closing couplet is awkward metrically, and the metaphor seems strained.

There are a few good poems here and there in Kerouac's works. The best are Haiku or gnomic. There is the essence of the blues in such a one as the 235th Chorus of *Mexico City Blues*: "How do I know that I'm dead/ Because I'm alive/ and I got work to do." Looking at #23 in *The Scripture of the Golden Eternity*, one can see this haiku-like verse has the element of surprise in its imagery that is basic to the moral communication of haiku: "Things don't tire of going and coming. The flies end up with the delicate viands." Kerouac's verse as a whole, though, suffers from spontaneity without inspiration. The result is verse that is tasteless and relatively insignificant.

In his essay "Essentials of Spontaneous Prose," Kerouac tells the would-be writer not to worry about exact words, just to pile them up, and make no revisions "except [for] obvious rational mistakes." He is told to "write outwards swimming in a sea of language to peripheral release and exhaustion." We are to bear in mind that the writer's own way is the only way for him; good or bad, it matters not, as long as he is honest, spontaneous, and confessional. He will be interesting because his work is not "crafted." Poetry, depending as it does upon making every word bear a burden of meaning, is ill-suited to this technique. In prose an unsure statement can be built on, explained further, gone over again, until meaning breaks through. The reader of prose will wait longer for meaning in what he reads. The confessional form in prose may be rambling, with experience recounted for its own sake, to some extent. Even so, Kerouac's critics assailed these tendencies in his prose. They said he had a tendency to treat everything that had happened to him as signficant and to mistake mere sensations for experience.

In the same essay he tells the novice to write as unconsciously as possible. He himself used benzedrine and marijuana to induce a state of semiconscious thought. He says to "write excitedly, swiftly, with writing-or-typing-cramps" in accordance with "laws of orgasm." "*Come* from within, out —to relaxed and said." The excitement of the writing depends, in his theory, upon the excitement of its creation, and that excitement is intensified not only through the writer's concentration but by the rapidity with which he writes. In his journals he always kept track of the number of words he managed to get down every day, and he was to tell Ann Charters much later, when she compiled a bibliography of his works, that he had written *On the Road* in three weeks (actually he had written only about a third of it in that time, using the famous roll teletypewriter paper to encourage his speed), that he wrote *Dharma Bums* in ten sittings, *Big Sur* in ten nights on a roll of shelf paper, and the most intense of his novels, *The Subterraneans*, in "three full moon nights of October."[13]

Speaking of his method of composition, Kerouac was to say, "The secret of narrative . . . is that you get hot when you get disgusted. That's the time not to stop. Just roll along."[14] The novel that shows his disgust at blazing heat is *The Subterraneans*. It is also his most successful use of spontaneous prose composition. *Time* magazine hit the key value of Kerouac's method when the reviewer noted: "*The Subterraneans*, in its tawdry, slapdash way, testifies to one of Kierkegaard's percepts: 'Life is not a problem to be solved but a reality to be experienced.' "[15] Written as a fast-paced series of recollections, one bit of memory piling in quickly on another, interrupting scenes with new recollections and then returning to the thread of narrative, the book has a nervous intensity that is sustained throughout. It is stylistically more of a piece than *On the Road*. It is also more unified in subject matter, being centered entirely on the anguish of a single interracial love affair.

Speaking of the prose of *The Subterraneans*, Kerouac describes it as "the prose of the future, from both the conscious top and the unconscious bottom of the mind, limited only by limitations of time flying by as your mind flies by with it."[16] By focusing on a central experience, he has channeled his outpouring of sensations into a meaningful, intense rush of prose. The "conscious top of the mind" has kept the focus essential to keep the experience within certain perimeters. This containment accounts for the *pressure* of confession that Kerouac communicates so well here.

In *On the Road, Visions of Cody, Big Sur*, and the other confessional narratives, the confession always takes the form of immediate escape—into the experiences of the road or into the random recollections of the mind. In *Visions of Cody* a series of scenes and short explanations of scenes, sometimes realistic, sometimes with distorted perception, comprise a great part of the book. One association triggers the next; sights, sounds, and smells of one place and time merge into another in the same sentence. Dreams, marijuana hallucinations, and real scenes alternate and merge without logic. Confession becomes confession without point, without logical end. It is a rehash of experiences for their own sake. They are often vividly presented but never developed, either analytically or with added layers of perception. As Seymour Krim noted quite trenchantly in his introduction to *Desolation Angels*, Kerouac generally adds spatially to his subject in his novels but adds little to deepen our view or to give us different perspectives (unlike Proust, to whom Kerouac sometimes liked to compare himself). At his best, though, Krim notes, he captures the texture and rhythm of his experience so that style and content become one.[17]

In an experimental piece, "Old Angel Midnight," Kerouac said he was trying to write a "spontaneous *Finnegan's Wake* with the sounds of the Universe itself as the plot and all the neologisms, mental associations, puns, word-mixes from various languages scribbled out in a strictly intuitional discipline at breakneck speed."[18] Reading the "narration," the critic is apt to see Kerouac's pronouncements as so much pretentious hogwash. Kerouac was no linguist. His puns are often just a babyish rearranging of word inflections, and his knowledge of foreign languages was limited to a highly imperfect knowledge of French (in spite of his ancestry) and a few words here and there in Spanish and maybe one or two other languages. The piece is nonsense and joyful fakery. Unlike *Finnegan's Wake*, it has no plan. It belongs with Kerouac's other *jeu d'esprit*, the script for *Pull My Daisy*.

Kerouac's Spontaneous Prose is best when it is kept within the bounds of a central focus. In *The Subterraneans* and in many single passages in his other works, he impresses the reader with his deep emotional need to communicate his experience. The rush of ideas, feelings, and images does not permit the cover-up of reason, and we see the conflicting forces in the personality of the confessor quite clearly. The strength of his emotions is communicated directly through the movement of his prose. It is worst when the focus is lost and the confession becomes an escape into fantasy and endless recapitulations of experiences that seem to have no tangible relation to one another. The author seems to have, in these instances, no urgent need to communicate at all. His mind is idling, and he is merely putting down words in the hope that what he is saying will actually trigger off some significant emotion.

Kerouac's lack of discrimination between "warming up" and "blowing deep" is a part of his confessional style, and like the jazz horn soloist he expects his audience to follow along with him through the bits of old blowing, riffs, and tentative stabs at a new theme, waiting for him to get "It," following the play of his mind. At times we are rewarded for our patient attentiveness; at other times it seems a tiresome exercise for both author and reader.

When the King of the Beats, as Seymour Krim called Kerouac, experimented with Spontaneous Prose, it was as a means of breaking with the "literary" writing which he felt strait-jacketed his expression. Henry Miller made his break with literary tradition in writing *Tropic of Cancer*, and James Joyce did it before him with *Ulysses*. Like those earlier iconoclasts, Kerouac was seeking a way of communicating the depths of his frustration with the modern world. He, like Miller and Joyce, felt he had to get beyond the bounds of conventional narrative to do it.

Spontaneous Prose was experimental and, as such, likely to be carried to excess and to be talked of as the writing of the future, just as every literary apostasy has been from Longinus's theories of the sublime to the Surrealist Manifesto of André Breton. Also, as with the earlier theories, Spontaneous Prose was very much a product of the literary situation extant. It expressed the Beat revolt against academia, against the New York critics, and the southern New Critics.[19] It complemented the artistic events of the time, what Krim calls "the insane playfulness, deliberate infantilism, nutty haikus, naked strip-teases, free-form chants and literary war dances of the Beats ..., a much-needed *release* against an authoritarian inhibiting-and-punishing intellectual climate that had succeeded in intimidating serious American literature."[29] Kenneth Rexroth speaks of the art movements of the time, the art of Charlie

Parker and of Jackson Pollock, and the poetry of Dylan Thomas as illustrating that "confabulation has come to determine structure." This movement toward organic form is the exact opposite of and a revolt against "the sterile, extraneous invention of the corn-belt metaphysicals or present blight of poetic professors," and he sees the Beats as carrying on that revolt.[21]

Kerouac was very much at the heart of things in San Francisco and New York in the late forties and throughout the fifties. He named the Beat Generation. He appears as a character, Gene Pasternak, in the first published Beat novel, John Clellon Holmes's *Go* (1952). He named Burroughs's *Naked Lunch* and Ginsberg's *Howl*. He also named a new little magazine, *Big Table*, when it came out in 1960.

Malcolm Cowley had read the manuscript of *On the Road* in 1950 and extolled Kerouac's talent in his own book *The Literary Situation*. In 1955 *New World Writing* published an excerpt from *On the Road*, which it titled "Jazz of the Beat Generation," under Kerouac's pseudonym, Jean-Louis. In the winter of that same year Kerouac published an excerpt from *On the Road* in *Paris Review*. The following year the excerpt "The Mexican Girl" was included in *The Best Short Stories of 1956*. Then, in 1957, Viking Press finally published *On the Road*. It was at the time, and it still is, *the* Beat novel, and 1957 is generally regarded as the height of the Beat literary movement. In 1962 *Big Sur* put an epitaph on the generation's literature, and the best of Kerouac's works were done.

In 1957 Lawrence Ferlinghetti, who along with Peter Martin had established City Lights Bookstore in San Francisco in 1955, was tried for selling an obscene book. The book was Ginsberg's *Howl*, and that trial indicated that the establishment was not bowing readily to the developing interest in the Beats. Three years later, in 1960, the chancellor of the University of Chicago forbade the distribution of the *Chicago Review* issue containing Kerouac's "Old Angel Midnight" and segments of Burroughs's *Naked Lunch*. Six of the seven student editors put out a new magazine, *Big Table,* the first issue of which contained the banned material. This issue was confiscated by postal authorities. These acts of censorship were roundly denounced by John Ciardi in the *Saturday Review.* Ciardi was one of Kerouac's severest critics, but he found some social value in both Kerouac's and Burroughs's works and felt they did not appeal to the prurient interest of the average man (social value and prurience being the principal legal tests for pornography at the time). Not only had the Beats, with Kerouac in the vanguard, won the respect of the New York publishers, but they had unwittingly engaged one of the nation's respected academics to plead their total right to be heard.[22]

Spontaneous Prose and like experiments by the Beats were, in a sense, legitimized by Ciardi's defense. Whether the critics liked them or not, they were seen as in some degree relevant to man's situation and a legitimate expression of his needs. Another defense had come earlier in a backhanded kind of way in Norman Mailer's *Advertisements for Myself* (1959). To the critics who complained that Kerouac and the Beats were not socially responsible and who condemned their nihilism, he noted that they were not, it was true, moving forward into collectivity but "backward to the nihilism of creative adventurers." In Mailer's view the destruction of order in art was necessary in order to get back to the fount of creativity, a fount that was not only the very essence of all expression but that was the basis of morality, the seat of man's instinctive sympathy with his fellows and his love of justice. Collectivity had proven to be totalitarian, and the random violence of the nihilist unleashing a spontaneous overflow of powerful feelings was, Mailer thought, better than the organized violence of the collective police state.[23]

Spontaneous Prose was supposed to allow the writer to point out things directly, concretely, one image after another, "no abstractions or explanations, wham wham the true blue song of man."[24] As E. E. Cummings had said in his lecture series at Harvard in 1952, it was necessary to "unthink" to get back to the basic, feeling self.[25] As William Carlos Williams had said, "No ideas but in things." The image direct—the essential expression of the creative impulse unclouded with interpretation or abstraction—was supposed to communicate the emotion of the writer to the reader more solidly than the more conventional methods of phrasing well–thought-out passages. Reading the continuous flow of Mailer's prose, a reader can see him reaching for the same sort of contact Kerouac is trying for, often with brilliant effect but also, as with Kerouac, with page after page of words rushing under the bridge of the reader's nose, giving only a sense of momentum promising another eventual crescendo. The reader tires of the ceaseless roar of thought unstopped, unmuted, and unchanneled. But to stop the words before they got out would be to run the risk of losing them altogether, of repressing the very emotion that the writer was trying to set free. Mailer and Kerouac both willingly sacrifice form for the momentary, powerful breakthrough of feeling and intuitive awareness that constitutes, for them, a higher reality not approachable through the rationally structured, conventional methods of composition.

In Mailer's *The Deer Park* (1955) the old professional writer, Charles Eitel, thinks of telling the younger writer, Sergius O'Shaugnessy, that the one thing that matters for the artist is that he find the real world "where orphans burn orphans and nothing is more difficult to discover than a simple fact," and that he then "blow against the walls of every power that exists" the trumpet of his defiance. Rexroth, speaking of Charlie Parker and Dylan Thomas, says that they communicated one central theme: "Against the ruin of the world, there is only one defense—the creative act."[26] In 1945 Kerouac said, "Life is my art . . ./ (Shield before death)/ Thus without sanction I live/ (What unhappy theodicy!)." And in the next stanza of this early poem, he says, "One knows not—/ One desires—/ Which is the sum."[27] The poem was written before he began preaching the sanctification of all men in the light of the Golden Eternity. It recognizes as Mailer's Eitel does, and as Parker and Thomas did, that the one positive force in a chaotic and negative world is the creative act. The form it takes is less important than the act itself and its constant repetition, a reaffirmation continually that the life-force is unquelled, that at least one sentient being is incorrigibly and undeniably aroused and compassionating. After one of his dreams of Allen Ginsberg, Kerouac tells us in his *Book of Dreams*, he woke up realizing with great certainty that sex and art (the two human creative acts) are life—"that or die" (p. 61). Spontaneous Prose is the celebration of the creative act; it is the creative act in progress. It invites the reader to be a part of the process, to stir up the kettle of old thought and experience, to inhale suddenly released aromas and to delight in the occasional whiff of inspiration that the whole process affords. If our view is that well-ordered formal art is impossible in the modern world, perhaps the creative act is all we can be sure of; and that we can know and feel its truth may be sufficient grounds for its repetitive celebration. Certainly, the dire fear that ultimately it too may be rationalized out of existence, along with God and the beneficent power of love, is some grounds for reassuring ourselves with its perpetual demonstration.

There were other reasons as well for Kerouac's adoption of Spontaneous Prose. He was fascinated by the way images would come unbidden into his mind. In *Visions of Cody*, he says, ". . . let us ascertain, in the morning, if there is a way of abstracting the interesting paragraphs of material in all this running consciousness stream that can be used as the progressing lightning chapters of a great essay about the wonders of the world as it continually flashes up in retrospect; as, for example, this night I ran cold water into a glass at the sink while everybody was high and immediately was reminded completely and perfectly of the cool exact waters of Pine Brook on a summer afternoon" (p. 258). Throughout *Visions of Cody* he indulges in random association and word play as though trying to conjure up the key memories and unifying images of his life, surprising them into consciousness, as it were.

To inspire these associations he took alcohol and drugs. He wrote *Visions of Gerard* while high on benzedrine, "Old Angel Midnight" while half-drunk on wine, and *Tristessa* while using both benzedrine and marijuana. Parts of other works too were written under the influence of one or more of these stimulants or depressants.[28] As early as November 1945 he was praising the mind-expanding qualities of benzedrine. In a letter to Allen Ginsberg he says, ". . . new material wells up like water following its proper level, and makes itself evident at the brim of consciousness. Brand new water!"[29] He also found, like the opium-taking Coleridge, that when his mind was stimulated by drugs the images of the mind took on such force that they seemed even more real than the facts of the physical world. As such, they seemed to possess a degree of truth that, if it could not be wholly understood, could not be easily denied. These images, the life in the stream of consciousness that he tapped, might well hold the key to his own spiritual existence, to the nirvana behind the veil of maya fact that he wanted to believe was illusion. Recording the images as they came, he could hope to capture for later study their connection, recurrence, and relationship to each other and to real events.

Kerouac extolled the painter Hugo Weber's "imaginary portrait" that started out as a painting of Ulysses S. Grant and "ended up as Edgar Allen Poe the drunkard of Baltimore and the Bronx," because it reflected the "simpleness of heart in the course of things" that is more important than exact reality in a frozen moment of time. To Kerouac the appearance is only a vague representation of the eternal reality, so the appearance is always modifiable in many different ways without making it any less true.[30] Like a child with a kaleidoscope, he watched the endless patterns of maya form and dissolve with wondering fear and delight. Much of his expression of what he sees seems to be a celebration of the mind-world creation, on the

one hand, and an attempt to hold the process on record, to hold
the patterns, in memory beyond change, on the other.

Spontaneous Prose is confessional by its very nature, and
confession came naturally enough to the Catholic-trained Kerouac. In fact, Kerouac attributed his confessional style directly
to his early Catholicism.[31] He looked upon confession as a
means to understanding and as a means of communicating
more truly than an artist could do through formal exposition.
In *Satori in Paris* he admits that he does not know how he
achieved his moment of enlightenment, but by telling the tale
of what he did and how he felt, he hopes to find out. He will,
he says, be fully candid, for "made-up stories and romances
about what would happen IF are for children and adult cretins
who are afraid to read themselves in a book just as they might
be afraid to look in the mirror when they're sick or injured or
hungover or *insane*" (p. 10). In these abnormal states there is
the possibility of overcoming the rote responses and of perceiv-
ing the world in a fresher and perhaps "truer" perspective. The
abnormal states are the ones that may give divine revelation.
In the candor of confession their meaning may be made clear,
their revelation made understandable and related to normal,
conscious reality.

The confession in some of Kerouac takes on the character-
istics of Henry Miller's surreal expressions of an emotional
state in his "Tropic" books, distorting the world of objects in
accord with the author's inner anguish. Speaking of the Lowell of his boyhood in *Doctor Sax*, the older Kerouac says, for
example, "—no notion there of the Lowell that came later, the
Lowell of mad midnights . . . , a burying of dirt, a digging up
of dirt, . . . axles full of grease lying in the river water and the
moon glinting in a rat's eye—the Lowell, the World, you find"
(pp. 10–11). The candor here is subjective, emotional, and not
at all reasoned and objective. Kenneth Rexroth compared Kerouac to Miller in this respect, saying that he was like Miller in
reflecting a world he really did not understand rationally and
that it was precisely because he felt it so deeply without being

able to dominate it through reason that he expressed himself with such "poignancy and terror."[32]

Kerouac's language bore the brunt of the critics' attacks on his use of Spontaneous Prose. Norman Podhoretz, in his article "The Know-Nothing Bohemians," remarks sarcastically about Kerouac and the Beats that for them "to be articulate is to admit that you have no feelings (for how can real feelings be expressed in syntactical language?), that you can't respond to anything (Kerouac responds to everything by saying 'Wow!'), and that you are probably impotent."[33] Paul Goodman says that among the Beats words like "crazy" and "the greatest" do not communicate anything except that the person saying them has had the experience, whatever it is, referred to by another.[34] Podhoretz, Goodman, Herbert Gold, and John Ciardi, to name only some of the more eminent critics of his work, all lamented what appeared to them to be a steadfast refusal to analyze, to dissect, to really understand the experience Kerouac was so rapidly recording.

Gold was particularly irritated with Kerouac's writing about such abstractions as Love, Life, and Death in *On the Road* without reference to concrete experience and deeper human emotion.[35] Spontaneous Prose seemed to encourage empty and repetitive philosophizing. And yet there are breakthroughs in thought that go beyond the empty abstractions, sudden grasps of central poetic images that convey a meaning to the senses and the intellect at once and that overcome the "dissociation of sensibility" that T. S. Eliot claimed was the curse of modern poetry. To illustrate the point, here is a sentence Ginsberg quotes from *Dharma Bums*: "Suddenly came the drenching fall rains, all-night rain, millions of acres of Bo-trees being washed and washed, and in my attic millenial rats wisely sleeping." According to Ginsberg, Kerouac has in this line "gone very far out in discovering (or remembering, or transcribing) the perfect patterns that his own mind makes, and trusting them, and seeing their importance—to rhythm, to imagery, to the very structure of the 'novel.'"[36]

In attempting to transcend the principles of "good writing," as taught at Columbia, with his movement into spontaneous, organic composition, Kerouac sacrificed order and form for what he thought of as a greater sense of life. He began in *The Town and the City* writing long accounts of boyhood experience in the manner of Thomas Wolfe, and when he moved into Spontaneous Prose he continued to regurgitate great chunks of experience, only now sensations and events, fact and feeling became more rushed together. The pace of the novels quickened at the expense of rational appreciation. The writer gives us a great sense of life under pressure, a sense of urgent anxiety that tells us his world is out of control and vibrating itself apart. His world is somewhat like the machine of the old order that cruelly slaughters its faithful servant in Kafka's "In the Penal Colony." Kerouac obviously expects his reader to feel his hero's plight as that of every man and to be awakened to his similarity of condition through the emotional charge of the author's nerve-connected prose. However, although his critics have found the charge of his prose undeniable, they have found it a poor substitute for the illumination and power provided by more sophisticated circuitry. They endlessly fault him for a lack of discrimination and for refusing to refine his sensations into meaningful experience.

The jazz idiom with which Kerouac and the Beats operated is, no doubt, in great measure responsible for his uninspired blowing as well as the occasionally ecstatic outbursts of poetic statement. His Catholic background and his interest in the work of the Black Mountain poets led him to a confessional style that mixes easily with jazz improvisation.

Above all, the Romantic belief that the seat of truth is in the basic human emotions makes of spontaneity a primary value. The Romantic writer believes the closer one comes to those emotions and the more purely they are communicated the more affecting will be his statement. Where the emotions are contained within the focus of a central subject, as in *The Subterraneans* and some parts of *Doctor Sax, On the Road,* and *Big Sur*, and are poured forth at a pace to match the concatenations of the aroused imagination of the writer, they are affecting. Where the focus is lost, they seem aimless, repetitive, and uninspired.

Kerouac was central to the Beat movement. His work may be looked at as an expression of Beat playfulness and a kind of Dadaist revolt against the literary critics and older forms of pre–World War II writing, including the proletarian literature of the 1930s. Much of his work is, like the film *Pull My Daisy* or the poetry of *Mexico City Blues*, an expression of the creative impulse very much for its own sake—a refusal of rules of creation and a celebration, in the act, of the spontaneity inherent in creativity.

In the final analysis Spontaneous Prose is spontaneous creation, an insight into the workings of the human mind, an attempt to get the reader into the act with the writer; and, finally, it is a way to record as rapidly as possible, thus presumably as freely and as completely as possible, life as an ongoing mental process. It assumes that the loss of discrimination, the abuses of language, and the lack of rational development are worthwhile sacrifices to the truth that lies locked within the heart, a truth that is emotional in nature and that can be unloosed only by circumventing the usual channels of formal art and human reason.

7

The New Romanticism

SINCE WORLD WAR II there has been a steadily growing Romantic movement in American letters. Basically, it has signified the refusal of youth to accept the limited role assigned to it by an adult middle class that bequeathed it a political legacy of atomic warfare, wars of containment, and cold-war purges in the name of patriotism; an economic legacy of eight-to-five employment, accumulation of material goods, and standardized suburban living; and the social legacy of the status of organization men, domestic boredom and divorce, and a loss of creativity and self-dependence. Refusing to accept the middle-class "realism" of their parents, the young have sought heroism, causes, religion, and, when these have seemed untenable, they have simply dropped out.

In place of institutions they look to the self. In place of custom they look to their own emotions. In place of sophistication they hold tightly to innocence. To grow into adulthood of the kind their parents have is a fearful prospect. If they are to grow at all, they will do so according to their own responses to life, and they are in no hurry. While rejecting the busy commerce of middle-class, industrialized society, they contemplate their own feelings, their own rapturous dreams and, perforce, their own sense of inadequacy. Like J. D. Salinger's children in the rye field, they are ever in danger of falling over that "crazy cliff"—into suicide, agonizing despair, or what the author suggests may be feared even more: insensitive, therefore "phony," adulthood.

None of these Romantic writers goes any further with the prophetic sense of doom than Kerouac. With Dean Moriarty in *On the Road*, life blurs into pure energy, annihilating all form. With Ray Smith in *Dharma Bums*, life recedes into Buddhistic staticity. Later, in *Big Sur*, with Jack Duluoz, it annihilates itself in fearful, drunken senselessness. Kerouac's apocalyptic vision is more steadfastly dreadful and uncompromising than that of any writer in this period that we could name. He is the Jeremiah of the tribe.

To see just how much others partook of the same vision as he and how they came to terms with it is better to understand the uncompromising quality of Kerouac's romantic ideals of heroism, poetic justice, and love triumphant. It is to define by contrast the sad limitations and poignant strengths of his vision. In looking at other writers who have, in one way or another, held a Romantic view in this period, we are then looking at Jack Kerouac in perspective.

The four writers chosen for this purpose are J. D. Salinger, James Purdy, John Knowles, and Ken Kesey. Salinger has been to middle-class high school students and college freshmen what Kerouac has been to the dropouts in Bohemia. His followers' view of life is troubled but not desperate. Their hopes for a piece of the American economic and social pie are still alive, although they question its flavor. Salinger, then, is chosen as a Romantic closer to the mainstream of our society, whose heroes nevertheless share the same fear as Kerouac's, that to move into adulthood in American society is to destroy oneself spiritually.

James Purdy is the most versatile of the writers chosen. *The Nephew* is a realistic novel, whereas many of his other works bear a close resemblance to the Theater of the Absurd in plot and in their compressed, stylized use of language and strikingly etched scenes. Nevertheless, through them all runs a strain of postwar romanticism that compares in several respects with the dominant Kerouac motif. It is, in fact, the interplay of the sense of hopeless absurdity in the human condition with a tenacious unwillingness to abandon the ideal of human triumph that makes the romanticism of our time at once more desperate and more touching, more unreal and more real than that of previous eras. We shall look at Purdy's work to see a complementary interplay of these two forces in the work of one who is more ready than Kerouac to accept the necessity of absurdity and the conditional qualities of love.

John Knowles is a writer whose concern with the movement of youth into a hypocritical and competitive adult world parallels Salinger's to some extent. But Knowles also emphasizes the importance of the individual's own code and the doubtful virtue of competition in ways that aid our assessment of the Kerouac characters' quest for self and escape from the social laws of competition and competitive judgment.

And in the writings of Ken Kesey, the last of the New Romantics to be considered here, we find the values of competitive individualism apotheosized in a way that Kerouac at one time would have wished for his hero Neal-Dean-Cody. The success of Kesey's Randle Patrick McMurphy and Hank Stamper is the success of the vital and the clever and is a marked contrast to the not-so-epic collapse of the Beat hero. The limits of the Kesey hero are reached in *Over the Border*, and the plight of Devlin Deboree underscores the descent into the maelstrom of Kerouac's Jack Duluoz.

J. D. SALINGER

Salinger began writing his stories about sensitive children adrift in middle-class America in the 1940s. His first Holden Caulfield story was sold to the *New Yorker* in 1941, but not published until 1946. By 1948 he was writing regularly for the *New Yorker,* and then in 1951 his landmark novel, *Catcher in the Rye,* appeared. Kerouac's *The Town and the City* had been published the previous year, and he was busy working on material that became *Visions of Neal* and *On the Road*.

As Warren French has pointed out, Salinger's heroes are always caught between the "phony" world of reality and the "nice" world they would prefer to live in.[1] The same is true of Kerouac's heroes, but in Salinger the "phony" world is eventually dealt with, whereas in Kerouac it is always rejected in favor of the ideal vision.

In *Catcher* there is growth in Holden Caulfield toward acceptance of human circumstance. Initially he wishes to be a catcher in the rye, keeping all the innocent children in the rye field from falling over the "crazy cliff" into perilous adulthood. However, he comes to realize as he watches his sister on the merry-go-round that children will grab for the brass ring, and their fall is a chance that must be taken. Although he condemns his teachers and fellow students as "phonies," he finds before long that he really misses them. His puerile perfectionism and self-centeredness give way to tolerance and love.

In *Franny and Zooey* (1961) Franny's disgust with her "phony" boyfriend and her disgust with vulgar audiences have caused her to retreat into a pursuit of mysticism. It takes her brother Zachary (Zooey) Glass to bring her out of her retreat. He does so by rejecting the way of Seymour, the child sensitive, who most resembled Kerouac's Gerard.

Zooey blames Seymour and Buddy Glass, his older brothers, for having tried to instill in the younger Glasses a sense of mystical beauty and goodness before they learned anything else. Their precocity, their fame as participants on the Wise Child quiz programs, and their early indoctrination into idealism made them into "freaks." Seymour himself was so sensitive that he would not come to his own wedding because he was "too happy." Unable to stand the world's ways, he eventually committed suicide. Such excessive idealism and sensitivity make one selfish, and Zooey knows it. He harangues his sister, telling her that her repetitive saying of the Jesus Prayer is a mockery of what Jesus stood for. What she needs to do is what she feels called to do, become an actress, and if she is superior to other people, she must realize that superiority incurs certain obligations. As Seymour said to Zooey when he refused to shine his shoes for an appearance on the quiz program when they were children, "Do it for the Fat Lady." The Fat Lady is every lump of humanity affected by one's actions, and, by extension, those lumps are part of Christ himself.

In Kerouac there is no counter to Gerard's sensitive idealism. Peter Martin and Jack Duluoz begin with their sensitive, mystic awareness of an ideal world of beauty and harmony and with the precocity that makes them believe in the power to effect its realization. The value of Gerard's saintliness is never questioned. In Kerouac there is no spokesman for growth and maturity, as there is in *Catcher in the Rye*. Although Holden initially rejects his Latin teacher's pronouncement that the mark of maturity is not looking for the noblest deed to do but living humbly to do what one can, we know, as adult readers, that this view is the very one Holden must eventually accept. Like Seymour and Holden at sixteen, Kerouac's heroes are perpetually shocked by hypocrisy and the lack of *caritas* in everyday life. They do not see that much of the phoniness and hostility they encounter is a response to their own selfish demands on others and a defense on the part of people whose egos are sensitive just like their own. The rest of the responses, Zooey would have us believe, is Fat Lady ignorance, and should be pardoned by those who regard themselves as generally superior to the ruck of mankind.

Between these two authors there is also a difference in religious point of view. In *Franny and Zooey* we see that the important values are truth to the self and sympathy and duty towards others. If one has these ethics, religion more or less takes care of itself. The quest for mystical union with Godhead is rejected when the way of Seymour is rejected. Both Kerouac and Salinger were attracted to Buddhism, but it is the Zen Buddhist compromise with the active world, which Kerouac rejected, that Salinger accepts.

Dan Wakefield sees "Teddy" as the only one of Salinger's stories in which the hero has a truly mystical experience.[2] Teddy feels that he has been reborn and that the death he prophesies at the hand of his sister is a fitting culmination for one who has finally had the ultimate illumination that "everything was God." He is now ready for nirvana. Along with his mysticism goes an ascetic's mistrust of women. He failed to achieve Brahma in his last incarnation, he says, because of a woman, and it is his sisters' jealousy of his spiritual superiority that he thinks will cause his early death. Kerouac's Jack Duluoz tries ascetic withdrawal in *Tristessa* and *Dharma Bums*, and although he waits in *Dharma Bums* for Avilokitesvara to carry him off, a kind of death wish, he soon lapses from mystic acceptance of the Infinite to a very physical and earthly boredom which makes him overjoyed to be leaving his mountain retreat and heading back to the life of the cities. Never going to the point of death, Kerouac's characters are always looking for ecstatic union, either through excesses of action or withdrawal.[3] That Salinger's most ascetic characters, Teddy and Seymour, end in accepting death may show that Salinger, although drawn to the possibilities of mystic experience, could see much better than Kerouac the life-denying character of the mystic's pursuit.

In Seymour and Teddy and in Leo Percepied and Jack Duluoz, there is also a morbid fear of the power of woman, symbol of fleshly instincts and desires, over the spiritual freedom of the male. The denial of the sex drive and the guilt felt when abstinence is broken or threatens to be broken lead Seymour to suicide, Leo Percepied to paranoia, Jack Duluoz to retreat into solitude or intoxication. The denial of life in certain of their characters is intimately connected with the denial of woman.

In "De-Daumier Smith's Blue Period" Smith is staring into a shop window at a girl dressing dummies with rupture trusses. Embarrassed, she falls down, and as she does so he is momentarily blinded by sunlight, only to find when he can see again that she is gone and in her place the floor is scattered with enameled flowers. This event is no mystic union with God-head. The flowers are flowers of love, the blinding flash of sunlight a sudden communication of love interest between two young people. As Josephine Jacobsen has described it, it is an exchange of "beatific signals" between boy and girl, destroying the sordidness of a world of dummies and rupture trusses.[4]

In "For Esmé—With Love and Squalor" Sergeant X quotes Father Zossima in Dostoevski's *Brothers Karamazov*: "Fathers and teachers, I ponder 'What is Hell?' I maintain that it is the suffering of being unable to love." Most of Salinger's stories are about restoring that capacity through bits of ecstatic communion between innocents (Holden and Phoebe, Smith and the girl in the window, the sensitive Sergeant X and the young girl Esmé, etc.) who reaffirm the possibility of love in a world of war and "phony" values. In his essay "The Rare Quixotic Gesture" Ihab Hassan has said, "It is much as if Salinger meant innocence to be, in our particular situation, the redemption of our ignorance."[5] In Kerouac the characters seldom show such innocent acts of love. The closest thing to such acts is the affair between Sal Paradise and the Mexican girl in *On the Road*, a situation in which love is tender and compassionate, undemanding, and sexually free and uncompli-cated. The love for Tristessa and the affair in *The Subterra-neans* are shadowed with guilt and self-recrimination, while Dean's and Cody's affairs lack the tenderness of the Salinger love relationships. The fact that Salinger's male-female rela-tionships are generally between children or an adult and a child (Seymour and his wife being the notorious exception) greatly diminishes the impact of sex against the bond of inno-cence. Kerouac's characters are generally older than Salinger's, and their contact with childhood is through memory. Even the child characters, Gerard, Peter Martin in *Town and the City* and *Vanity of Duluoz*, and Jack in *Doctor Sax*, express a nostalgic view that is mournful with the author's knowledge that childhood cannot come again. Unable to accept the adult world, Kerouac's young characters slip off into mysticism (for example, Dean's and Sal's quests for ecstasy, Jack's "husk of doves" in *Doctor Sax*, and Jack's "vision" of Gerard), whereas Salinger's characters hold to their relationship with the younger children and learn to assume an adult responsibility for the preservation of an intuitive, aware, and loving response to life in them and in themselves.

Seymour is the cardinal exception here. In "A Perfect Day for Bananafish" his interest in the young girl on the beach is a diversion from the torment of adult responsibility and marriage. He is her protector in the ocean, and he kisses the arch of her foot like the chivalric knight he might wish to be. Rather than move from dreams of purity and innocence to sophistication and carnal release, from carefree fantasy to day-to-day domestic life, he chooses suicide. His fear of sex is shown in Freudian symbolism in his tale of the bananafish which go into a hole, eat too much, and swell up and cannot get out again and so starve to death.

William Wiegand, in his article "Seventy-eight Bananas," says that Holden and Seymour both suffer from banana fever, that they are surfeit with sensation and unable to discriminate.[6] Hypersensitivity to life is the curse of the sensitive child-innocent in both Kerouac and Salinger. In Kerouac the lack of discrimination is a fault made into the virtue of acceptance and potential knowledge of the All. In Salinger it is treated as a virtue insofar as it permits a wide-eyed view of the way things are, disclosing the "phoniness" of the adult world; but when Holden is forced to make a choice between running away and possibly ruining his sister's life in the process and decides to stay, and when he admits he misses his schoolmates, he is beginning to discriminate in his feelings toward the world around him. Some attractions, some loyalties and needs, are greater than others and are worth preserving in spite of having to submit to the jurisdiction of parents who do not understand him and the general repulsiveness of some of his Pencey school-mates. Seymour's problem is, as Zooey tells us in *Franny and*

Zooey, that he swallowed too much philosophic idealism and that in his generalized love of mankind and his code of responsibility for his family he has failed to establish any kind of really close I-thou love relationship with anyone. He remains throughout the mysterious older brother, more a product of Buddy Glass's need for a hero to worship than a flesh and blood sibling.[7] In this respect Seymour and Kerouac's Gerard are much alike.

In style there is no lack of discrimination in Salinger. Every word is well chosen in *Catcher*, and the failure of the informal narration in *Seymour, an Introduction* is less a failure in discrimination than in focus. The author seems tired of Seymour, and Buddy Glass, his narrator, seems to express the author's confusion as to whether or not Seymour is really as believable as he wants him to be. If Zooey turns out to be a preacher at the end of *Zooey*, and if we find his sermon too long and Franny's acceptance too pat, the importance of certain events and the emphasis on what Salinger wishes to say are seldom in doubt. Salinger was not trying to "get it all in," and he never attempted to capture the rush of sensations as Kerouac did.

Salinger's *New Yorker* style is not only tighter and more focused than Kerouac's, but it evinces a greater degree of authorial detachment. It is true that at times Salinger becomes somewhat sentimental over his characters, but overall he tends to see them ironically. Holden will learn how to conduct himself with women one of these days, but for now he is an awkward and impotent would-be lover. One both pities and is amused at his awkwardness. Even in such a story as "A Perfect Day for Bananafish," the somewhat sentimentalized Seymour is shown to be not only right in his kindness to children but wrongfully rude when he takes offense at an imaginary slight put upon him by a woman's supposedly sneaking a look at his feet (a sign actually of his own morbid feelings of sexual inadequacy, when we consider that he has made the foot of the child a substitute love object for his own bride).[8]

We are seldom allowed to smile at Kerouac's heroes. The closest we come to a Salinger-like detachment is in Ray Smith's eventual disgust with his asceticism both in the sex episode and in his leaving the mountain in *Dharma Bums*. That novel is the high point of overall perspective for Kerouac.

In both novelists there is a distrust of logic and society's use of words for communication. The reiterated "Wow!" in Kerouac, the half-sentences and rambling phrases of Dean Moriarty, and the substitution of sense impressions for thought have their counterpart in Holden Caulfield's "People never notice anything." Teddy's desire to have children vomit up all the apple of logic that they have eaten, to restore them to an innocent, fully sensate way of viewing things without preconception also suggests that feeling is more important than logic or words. Both see the reality of life and communication between individuals as dependent not upon words but upon signs ("beatific signals"). In Salinger the signals are most often between individuals; in Kerouac they are more often emanations of God in the abstract.

Each sees the need to circumvent the usual thought-patterns of response to know love. In Kerouac love is the compassion of those who share a common frustration, a thwarted heroism or thrust toward Godhead; or, as in *The Subterraneans*, it is the paternal pity that excuses carnal lust. Seldom is it the innocent abandonment that we find in the Mexican girl episode in *On the Road*. In Salinger love is innocent compassion, as it is in the girl's gift to Sergeant X in "For Esmé—With Love and Squalor," Holden's gift of a carousel ride to Phoebe, or Boo Boo Tannenbaum's imaginative play with her child in "Down at the Dinghy." Above all, in Salinger love is *caritas*; it is a deeply felt, honest expression of responsibility. The message Zooey delivers to Franny in the last of Salinger's novels is that love is based on truly being able to see another's situation from his point of view and that love in the abstract means very little. When Holden is asked if he will buckle down and study when he returns to school, he says it is a silly question, for he will not know until he does it. He must *feel* that compulsion to be truly responsible, and that *feeling* will only come with expanded identification with others, his family, his teachers, and his schoolmates. In Kerouac, although there is talk of *caritas*, the characters are generally too self-concerned, too inward in their experience of life, to really feel responsibility for other specific people for more than a few fleeting moments. Kerouac's people are always on the edge of despair. Salinger sacrifices a couple to their own visions of calamity in Teddy and Seymour, but for the most part the others pull back from the brink by broadening their perspective on themselves and the rest of society and by developing a genuine empathy for the lives of others.

JAMES PURDY

After publishing a book of stories in Great Britain at his own expense and being favorably reviewed by Dame Edith Sitwell and other British critics, midwesterner James Purdy began drawing critical attention in his native America in the late 1950s. When *Malcolm* was published in 1959, he was heralded by many British and American reviewers for his mastery of a finely honed prose style and his treatment of man's absurd condition in the contemporary period.

As in Kerouac's books, Purdy's youthful heroes tend to hold to the innocent vision of childhood at all costs. Their arrested development is due to their being in a world which has no central authority or order, symbolized by the loss or failure of the father. In this respect there are definite parallels between *Malcolm* and other Purdy works, and Kerouac's Lowell novels. In *Malcolm* the fifteen-year-old boy sitting on the golden bench across the street from the hotel is waiting for his father. In order to get him into life, the astrologer, Cox, gives him a list of addresses to call at. In the process of his calls he learns from the love-hate relationship between a midget and his wife (with many white moles) and between a business magnate, Girard Girard, and his wife (who loves him for his name) that love is a difficult business and married love the strangest kind of all. When he himself finally marries Melba, a jazz singer, she makes such heavy sexual demands on him that she helps him to an early grave. His most satisfying relationship is in his short time with Melba's Negro motorcyclist friend, Gus, who is to "mature him up," at Melba's request, by getting Malcolm drunk, having him tattooed, and getting him to bed with a whore. Having completed the overseeing of Malcolm's traditional sailor's initiation, Gus, whose own dissipation has worn him out, dies. The initiation is useless with the substitute father's death. Malcolm goes up to a man in a lavatory who he says is his father and is repulsed. His own death is imminent after that, for Malcolm cannot make his way into the adult world without the support, love, and guidance of the father in life or in heaven, and Malcolm is not religious.

The absurdity of Malcolm's situation is underscored by his initial position in the novel, where, like Samuel Beckett's characters in *Waiting for Godot*, he appears to be waiting for an authority (the father) to appear once again, and by his activity, which is no more sensible than the antics of Vladimir and Estragon. After Malcolm's death the astrologer finds another boy, who outdoes Malcolm by going to even more addresses before his demise. His absurdity is carried out a bit longer. Like Beckett, Purdy appears to be telling us that man lives in a world with no purpose but to endure. His world is one in which human relationships are essential but mostly unsatisfying and in which love is not lasting, nor without hostility.

In Kerouac's work, when innocence is about to be lost, the character leaps into a life of sensation or withdraws into Buddhistic contemplation. In Purdy the boy character stares in wonder at what he sees, uncomprehending, uninvolved, only doing what he is told, until his inner longing for love and a harmonious human relationship becomes so big a sorrow it chokes him to death. The characters who lean toward religion in Purdy, notably the young boy Claire in *63: Dream Palace* and Jethro in *Jeremy's Version*, are regarded as pitiable rather than as models, like Kerouac's saintly Gerard. Their morality is not for this world of impossible choices. In the short story "Plan Now to Attend" Graitop, leader of the New Religion, is gotten drunk by an alcoholic salesman; and, condescending to the youthful-looking Graitop's innocence, the salesman puts him to bed and kisses him goodnight. In the story "Sermon" God suggests that the people are too jaded, too continuously without vision to change their lot. They are hopeless and the God they know is a mistake. He is also the God they deserve. He is as tired of them as they of Him.

In her book of essays on Purdy's work, *The Not-Right House*, Bettina Schwarzschild has noted how often the character is faced with a moral dilemma.[9] In *63: Dream Palace* Claire's older brother, Fenton, has to choose between life as a kept man and loyalty to his pure, angel-haired little brother, who will not leave the strange house in the slums that they had given to them. Claire is apparently murdered, whether by Fenton or by another is not clear, but the hostility in Fenton's heart is enough symbolically to lay waste the innocent morality of an alter ego. For Fenton would like to be independent and pure, but his basic needs for food, comfort, and attention demand that he allow himself to be used by others, as a homosexual's lover or an old woman's young husband. In *Jeremy's Version* Jethro hates his mother for being a whore and longs for the authority of a father. When his own father, Wilders Fergus, returns, Jethro finds that the father's power is only effective in terms of physical force, when he bests a man in a fight. In the modern world the father, in this case, is one who cannot handle his money and whose good intentions always lead to disaster. In the end, after half-trying to shoot his mother, Jethro is forgiven by her but told that she is penniless and cannot take him. Resentful at one time of her lovers and her attentions to an older brother, he now finds no substitute for her love under the harsh discipline of a maiden aunt and no direction from a father who is dependent now upon the aunt's largesse. He can neither stay in the womb nor move into adulthood. Like Malcolm, he is stymied and enervated.

In Kerouac, Jack Duluoz finds a refuge with Memère when all else fails. In Purdy the mother is no substitute for the father or for satisfactory sexual relations. She is most apt to be at war with the very being that the boy wants to become. In "Why Can't They Tell You Why" the mother orders her son to burn a box of pictures he has of his lost father. To burn the pictures is to burn Daddy, and he refuses, collapsing on the floor in gut-tearing anguish. Though to some degree Madame Girard and Melba attempt to mother Malcolm, they do not assuage the pain of his father quest. Nor does Rick, Elvira's older son in *Jeremy's Version*, remain with Elvira when he has a chance to have a career in the theater. He is sick of helping to support her and tired of her smothering love. He achieves the break that Jethro cannot.

In *Cabot Wright Begins* Cabot has raped over three hundred women out of sheer boredom. Most of them seem to have enjoyed experiencing the thrust of Cabot's "nine inch sword." He is, however, finally jailed and then eventually released to begin his life over again. Life in the commercial world, as a general partner in a stock brokerage, loss of his adoptive parents, and his wife's insanity sent him on his sexual binge. His encounter with the law has taken care of his sexual prowess, however. All his life he has only been able to giggle instead of laugh, but after confessing what he can remember of his early life to Zoe Bickle, the publisher's ghost writer, he finds that he can laugh heartily at the meaninglessness of it all. His laughter purges him of all feelings of guilt, and now perhaps he is ready to "begin," to live without undue expectation in an absurd world. Just how long the hero could endure in a state of self-acknowledged impotence and insignificance we cannot be sure. Purdy's other heroes (Malcolm, Amos, Jethro) either die or are on their way out once that stage is reached. The laughter of the absurd is only a momentary release, after all.

Man must have his visions, his reason, if not "to be" at the moment, then to continue his being, some yearnful hope which he hardly dare admit, some sense that Godot may, after all, finally appear. For Kerouac, the answer lay in the ecstasy of sensation and a mystical vision of nirvana beyond the absurdities of maya.

In both authors sex is most often a release from boredom, though in Purdy homosexuality is most often the only means the character has in a world of estranged parents and general selfishness of establishing human love. Homosexuality is acceptable in both authors as an expression of love and compassion but hateful where one partner exploits the other, as is the case in the sadistic actions of Captain Stadger and the masochistic martyrdom of Daniel Haws in Purdy's *Eustace Chisholm and the Works*. Eustace says that Haws is chicken-hearted in not allowing a homosexual relationship with the yearning young Amos, and Haws pays dearly for his love of Amos and his guilt. Looking for an ecstasy of love, Stadger tortures Haws to death and commits suicide. In the case of Bernie Gladhart, in *Cabot Wright Begins*, after discovering that his book about Cabot Wright will not be published, and also discovering that no one really thinks he can write, a homosexual relationship with a Congolese Negro is restorative. In *The Nephew* it is Cliff's relationship with the homosexual Vernon Miller that apparently gave him the only feeling of being respected and attended to that he had had in his entire life.

As in Kerouac's *Pic*, Purdy's uncommercialized Negroes are treated as good-hearted, instinctive beings, free of the white man's guilts and compulsions. Winters Hart, the Congolese in *Cabot Wright Begins*, says he wants no part of the black man's America if it means becoming white; and when Bernie tries to rationalize their relationship, he tells him to enjoy it and stop talking. Words would only falsify it and create psychological problems. Gus, in *Malcolm*, is one who takes life as it comes, and whose relatively disinterested kindness is quite the opposite of the whites'.

The idea that marriage is the only normal sexual condition is heavily satirized in *Cabot Wright Begins* in the therapy clinic episode with Dr. Bugleford, a reformed pervert who is now fanatically trying to eliminate perverts by either marrying them or annihilating them. Throughout Purdy's works the married state (in the cases of the Raphaelsons in *Malcolm*, the Ferguses in *Jeremy's Version*, the Chisholms in *Eustace Chisholm*, and couples in his short stories such as "Don't Call Me by My Right Name") is parlous indeed. Love is precious in Purdy, and one should savor it where one can find it and not spoil it with unnecessary attention to custom or inhibition. The attitude in Kerouac and the Beats is similar, of course, but the Beat characters' relationships are seldom as intense as they are in Purdy. The characters in Kerouac are looking beyond love to destiny and Godhead; in Purdy they are principally trying to find and hold love itself.

As in the writing of the Beats, there is in Purdy a strong aversion to the commercial values of our society. In *Jeremy's Version* the financially successful Warburton discovers that he believes in nothing except football and other sports that show competition at its best. He believes that love is a masquerade for human selfishness. He finds relief only in work and competition. The same is probably true of the more elegant Girard Girard in *Malcolm*, who has only the most casual alliances with wives and others, and who says sagely that love means only what money and power tell it to mean. In Purdy, as in Kerouac, the youthful heroes refuse to follow the way of commercial society. They see it as corrupting love, art, and personal integrity.

In both Kerouac and Purdy there is a distrust of the spoken word for communicating honest feeling. In Kerouac much is made of getting "It," a knowing beyond words, and words are often used in his poetry to show how little words can convey, how little we can logically know. The ecstatic speech of Neal-Dean-Cody conveys excitement often without meaning. Words are often merely the expression of sensation. In Purdy the relationship between Bernie Gladhart and Winters Hart in *Cabot Wright Begins* is not reducible to words. In *The Nephew* the bickering between brother and sister, Boyd and Alma Mason, covers a silent love and sympathy that comes to the fore when Boyd has his stroke and Alma knows of Cliff's death. The depths of Fenton's conflicting feelings toward his little brother in *63: Dream Palace* are likewise not expressible except in symbolism, the tender act of burial in the old chest in the attic and the loving curse in Fenton's one-line benediction.

In Purdy, however, language is often shown to be inadequate simply because there is no attention. In the general lack of *caritas* no one feels, no one listens. In "Daddy Wolf" the depressed veteran who has lost his wife dials phone numbers at random to tell his story to someone. In "Home by Dark" the generation gap is too broad, and the grandson gives up on his grandfather and lets him talk only about the innocent things the grandfather believes belong to childhood.[10]

Because the characters have such a difficult time making any kind of impression on one another in Purdy, their sense of loneliness is very acute. Malcolm bounces off the other characters in the novel without making a lasting impression and dies, soon to be forgotten. Cliff in *The Nephew* never felt that anyone really "treated" him until Vernon Miller came along. Until Zoe Bickle listens to his story, Cabot Wright is unable to derive the benefits of confession, although he has, while being beaten by the police, told them many stories about his escapades. The lack of communication is tied to a lack of *caritas*, a loss of humanity, and the frustration of love in nearly all of Purdy's work.

In the use of noncommunicating speech, of the isolated character in the midst of society and the ineffectual father-God, and of the rather bizarre descriptions of character and scene, Purdy's work bears a close relationship to the work of Beckett, Ionesco, Pinter, Albee, and others of the Theater of the Absurd. *Malcolm* was, in fact, adapted for the stage by Edward Albee. On the other hand, *The Nephew* is more a traditional treatment of small-town life, with solid characters and realistic human relationships.

Purdy's style is never as loose as Kerouac's. In *Malcolm* the economical, precise wordage is what makes the work move cleanly and emphatically from one preposterous situation to the next. Since the writing of that work in 1959, Purdy has loosened up his style somewhat so that in *Jeremy's Version* (1970) there are a fair amount of verbosity and patches of trite phraseology, partially accounted for by the use of a melodramatic narrator, Uncle Matt Lacey. Like Salinger in *Seymour, an Introduction*, Purdy seems to be trying for a freer narrative style in this last work, and because of the richer material he does succeed better than Salinger in developing character and keeping his reader's attention.

JOHN KNOWLES

In his first novel, *A Separate Peace* (1960), John Knowles expanded his earlier story "Phineas" into a larger statement of the child's innocent vision, which is so central to the works of Kerouac and other Romantic writers of our time. Knowles, a graduate of Exeter and Yale, turned to his knowledge of prep school life for the basic frame of "Phineas" and *A Separate Peace*; but he went much further imaginatively in the creation of Phineas (Finny), his innocent idealist.

In the novel Phineas is an original and a natural. He is a "D" student who is unconcerned about his grades. He is a natural athlete who is not fiercely competitive. When he breaks the school swimming record, it is privately with only his friend Gene Forrester in attendance, and then he swears Gene to secrecy. He is keen on seeing what he can do, how far he can go, what talents he has and how he can use them, but he desires no great acclaim and has no desire to win out over anyone else. His view of sports is that everyone wins. Competition is merely a means of developing one's own abilities; which team wins the game is inconsequential. He innocently extends this view of sports to the war that is going on in the world beyond the playing fields of Devon School.

Because he is a natural athlete, he assumes that his friend Gene Forrester is a naturally good student and does not need to study to get his grades. Gene comes to resent Finny's intrusions on his study time; when Finny insists that they climb a tree and perform a double jump together as a sign of their courage and comradeship, Gene is so provoked that he shakes the limb, causing Finny to fall to the ground and break a leg. Gene has looked at Finny in his own terms, believing that Finny was jealous of his success as a student and that he was trying to lower his grades by taking him away from his books. When he finds out that Finny had no such intent, he is contrite and allows the fallen athlete to displace his own dreams upon him, letting Finny train him for the Olympics. Ironically, the only Olympics that Gene participates in are the ones concocted by Finny at the winter carnival, a mock-Olympics in which the skiers jump off three-foot slopes. The Olympics end in a snowball fight in which Finny makes a sham of the rules so that nobody wins.

Finny refuses to let Gene tell him of his guilt; but Brinker, the class organization man, insists that the facts be brought out, and Phineas hears Gene's confession. Finny then admits that although he has mocked the war ever since his injury, calling it a false war trumped up by old men to keep the young under their control, he has mocked it only because he now knows that he cannot enter it. Finny forgives Gene his act of unpremeditated anger and dies. Gene, at the end, feels "Phineas-filled," having learned by Phineas's example to love forgivingly and to live for what one can be unto oneself without the compulsion to win out over others at the cost of unkindness and injury.

Phineas is in many ways Gene Forrester's Gerard. Like Jack Duluoz's older brother, who died young, he espouses kindness toward all things. He cannot go on living in a world in which the survival of the fittest is law. His death is a symbolic message to the surviving soul-mate to strive for something higher than the commonly accepted laws of human behavior. He is also somewhat like Dean Moriarty, a natural athlete; and, like Dean's play on the basketball court, his play is for the sake of seeing what the individual can achieve unto himself. Both Kerouac and Knowles see the warring competition of our society as a curse upon the human values of kindness and comradeship and a block to the enjoyment of animal grace, the beauty of our instincts free of fear and hostility.

Phineas's view of the war is innocent to begin with—he thinks of it as an extension of play. When he cannot compete he declares his separate peace, but neither the first vision of war nor the peace that he declares can remain unclouded in the face of what war is and the real nature of men who produce it. When Leper returns from battle to tell Gene the horrors of the real thing, the innocence of the Devon playing-field view of war, of life, is shattered. A Phineas cannot survive in such a world; but Gene Forrester, since he has the darker forces of war within him and knows them as Phineas never did, can. With his spirit informed by the innocent vision of Phineas, he can not only survive but possibly control the fear and hostility that corrupt men's potential for love and goodness. Gene has absorbed Christ's (Finny's) message for earthly man without escaping into mysticism, more in the manner of Zooey Glass than Jack Duluoz.

Phineas is an emblem of courage and love. He has the courage to go his own way, to dare to extend his limits athletically, and the courage to love and to forgive. He does not love everyone; but when one has demonstrated a predominance of courage, loyalty, and honesty, Phineas extends to him love and forgiveness for the occasional lapse of virtue. His love is dependent upon the cardinal value of courage, as it was for Ernest Hemingway's heroes.[11] And it is this relationship of values that is the nexus upon which the action of Knowles's second novel, *Morning in Antibes* (1962), depends.

Nicholas Bodine finds that he cannot run away from his

marriage. His wife follows him to the Riviera, where he has gone to recuperate from the strains she has put upon him with her recurrent love affairs. When he rejects her overtures for a new beginning, she takes up with a masochistic Frenchman who she feels will profit emotionally from her compulsion toward promiscuity. Unable to leave her to fate, Nicholas gains his courage and forcefully reclaims her as his wife. In the end he admits that love hardly ever conquers, but it fights. His inability to let go of Liliane is similar to hero Dick Diver's inability to amputate himself from the psychotic Nicole Warren in F. Scott Fitzgerald's *Tender Is the Night*, which was also set on the Riviera. She is the bone of his bones (as Scott once said of Nicole's prototype, his wife Zelda Sayre Fitzgerald) and one who is vulnerable, who needs him in spite of herself. Unlike the emotionally bankrupt Dick Diver, however, he finds the courage to pull her back to save her from herself and to save himself from total self-revulsion.

As with Gene Forrester, the hero of *Morning in Antibes* is shown the way by a kind of code hero, a young Arab servant of his, Jeannot, who is basically honest, loyal, kind, and courageous, who has helped him when he was sick, is grateful for employment, and who in the end is going to Algeria to avenge his father's death at the hands of French parachutists.

Over all the characters hang the war clouds of the Algerian revolt. Antibes is naturally one of the most beautiful spots on earth, but the town is corrupted by its gamblers, black marketeers, and its paranoid attitudes toward the Arabs. The rich Frenchman who wishes to marry Liliane cannot live down his past as a Petainist during World War II; he prizes nothing but excellence, he says, and would exterminate the Arabs. He is the War-God and Competitor writ large, so hateful of weakness that he hates himself at base more than anyone else. Jimmy Smoot, whose American millionaire father won the spoils which support him, is a foolish rich boy, fearful of the impending war and of going home without a career. He has taken up photography with a German camera he does not know how to operate. He fails in love with his European fiancée because of his lack of trust and because he really has no feeling to communicate except his fear of being alone. Once again Knowles shows that Darwinian competition corrupts both love and integrity, and, contrary to the ethic of *laissez faire*, it actually ruins man's chances for self-realization.

In Kerouac's *The Subterraneans* the love affair is more intensely described than it is in Knowles's book, largely because of the nervous, high-pitched prose style of the Beat author as opposed to the more understated presentation of Knowles. Knowles's message too gets in the way of characterizations. Liliane, the *femme fatale*, is more a frail wisp of the hero's fancy than a vibrant emotion-charged human being, although Knowles continually assures us that she is deeply passionate and strong because of her passionate energy. Kerouac's Mardou Fox is a better representation in this respect of what Liliane is supposed to be. Kerouac, moreover, is not trying to make courage an absolute and does not force his character to any heroic excesses in reclaiming his love. As a confession of guilt and a failure of courage in love, Kerouac's is the more honest work.

In *Indian Summer* Knowles juxtaposes an Irish Catholic millionaire's son with WASP values against his old school chum, a one-quarter American Indian whose values are natural and instinctive. Neil Reardon does not learn from Cleet Kinsolving as Gene does from Phineas or Nicholas from Jeannot, and in the end Cleet throws off WASP dominance altogether by raping Neil's security-loving wife and abandoning Neil to his Irish Catholic sex guilt and WASP ideology.

M. E. Mengeling has noted the Dionysian and Apollonian opposition in *A Separate Peace* in his article "*A Separate Peace*, Meaning and Myth,"[12] but Nietzsche's mythological outline of the forces in human tragedy is even more clear-cut in *Indian Summer*. Neil Reardon is intellectual, adopts the millionaire liberal's position on all matters, and hates all people who are not children because they pose a threat to his authority

and status. His instincts are controlled by his father's dicta of
diligence, responsibility, strength, determination, and success.
Cleet, on the other hand, knows only that he wants to fly and
dreams of establishing an airline in Alaska. When he finds
that the Reardons will not support that idea and that they look
upon him as one who needs their paternal care because he is
not bright and his father was a friend of Neil's father, he re-
volts. His stupid, Indian look is a refusal to sham what he does
not feel and a sign of his stoic ability to endure in spite of social
convention and dominance of the WASP. Above all, he is
"healthy," giving rein to his powerful and honest instincts,
raping Neil's wife only because she secretly wants to be raped
and he senses it and because he needs to make his own decla-
ration of independence.

As Nietzsche noted in *The Birth of Tragedy*, it is the im-
balance of the Dionysian and Apollonian natures in man that
makes his lot an unhappy one. We can be sure that the future
of both Neil Reardon and Cleet Kinsolving will be fraught
with frustrations, but of the two the Dionysian Kinsolving is
the heroic one, because he is faithful to his inner self at all
costs, because he dares against the odds, against reason, to try
to become the fullest possible emanation of his instinctive desires. Neil Reardon, on the other hand, subordinates his instinctive, daring, childhood self to the conventional expectations of
his father's class—that is, order, security, and dominance at all
costs.

In *The Paragon* (1971) Knowles's hero is a young eccentric at Yale. Louis Colfax has a photographic memory, a wide
variety of interests, including oceanography and perpetual motion, and a highly keyed nervous system that makes him both
sensitive and impulsive. Knowing that he feels more deeply
than most and that his intellectual interests and impulsive actions are most often disturbing to others, he feels very isolated.
With the failure of his love affair with his pagan love, Charlotte, and his being thrown out of the marines "for the good of
the service," he fears that he may be a failure. Within his fam-

ily are a number of warped persons who failed to realize their potential and became paranoid, alcoholic, or in some other way stunted.

Colfax, like Cleet Kinsolving and Phineas, is a loner. His only steadfast friend is the colored intellectual on the campus, the Afro-Brazilian Marxist Clement Jonaz, who lives sufficiently beyond the pale himself to be tolerant of Colfax. Like Nicholas Bodine, he concludes that his love failed because he did not trust it enough. Charlotte marries a producer and has a child (which Colfax assumes to be his own), and out of desperation he kidnaps the child, giving it up only when he finds that it really needs a woman's care. He feels the failure in love has scarred him but takes solace in the belief that through his intellectual pursuits he can make some sort of offering to the world, an offering that will prove his love for it and gain its recognition and trust.

Both Cleet and Lou Colfax are saved by their vision of a career that will satisfy their most powerful need for respect. In Kerouac's work Sal Paradise and Jack Duluoz, as writers, envision the same saving end, but for them it is not enough. In spite of Jack Duluoz's statement that if he could surround himself with all the books in the Duluoz Legend from beginning to end he could die happy, his inflated quest for apotheosis doomed him to unhappiness. Except among some of his associates and younger readers, Kerouac himself and his fictional counterparts were not regarded as respectable prophets of the Way nor, certainly, as the writer-heroes of the larger society that they envisioned.

Fortunately for the hopes he represents, Knowles has stopped in his treatment of the isolated, young hero at a point where the vision is as yet untried. Cleet is just breaking away from the Reardons' dominance at the end of the novel, and Lou is just beginning to reconcile himself to a stoic intellectualism when the action stops in *The Paragon*. Success for the slow-thinking Cleet and the scientific visionary, Lou, seems dubious at best. Yet, with faith in their goal, they are better off than Kerouac's Neal-Dean-Cody, whose attempts to be anything specific are cut short by the character's own fear of failure, his impetuousness, and his quest for ecstasy. In the last analysis both Cleet and Lou remain believers in the American Dream. The Neal Cassady characters, spawned out of a failed parenthood, a reform-school education, and without any measurable success by any social standards, do not. As the great American hero, Neal-Dean-Cody is a flop; as the great American anti-hero, he is in the running along with such contemporary characters as William Faulkner's Joe Christmas, Saul Bellow's Tommy Wilhelm, and John Updike's Rabbit Angstrom.

In his last two novels Knowles seems to suggest that the quest for heroic attainment is worth the high risk of failure. That failure is most likely in a warring and competitive society such as our own is amply shown in his first novel, *A Separate Peace*, in the fates of Leper and Phineas. In his book *Double Vision* (1964) Knowles looks at America from the vantage point of a tour abroad and finds it too comfortable, too slick, and too scheduled, too Reardonish, if you will. It is also not a country that will point the way to a revivification of religious or ethical values. Yet, he is able to conclude in the last of the travel essays that comprise this book that America does offer its citizens more chance for personal freedom and self-development than do the other cultures.[13] This perspective accounts for the more optimistic view of the American hero's struggles in *Indian Summer* (1966) and *The Paragon* (1971).

Nevertheless, like Thomas Wolfe almost thirty years before, Knowles sees from his bifocal viewpoint that one of the prices we pay in America for our individualism is a great sense of loneliness, born of a weak sense of community and the individual's search for his place in the sun. Kerouac paints Neal and Jack in that situation in the chain of novelistic portraits extending down the road from *On the Road* to *Big Sur*. In Kerouac's last novel the nostalgia for the lost community of Lowell, the bitterness over the failure of the father, and the plea for religious assurance suggest that the quest for earthly

success in America is doomed, the American dream mere-
tricious.

In his last novel, *Spreading Fires* (1974), Knowles has
gone back to Antibes for his setting and a further development
of the theme of love. In this novel the Canadian manservant's
guilt over his homosexuality rivals that of James Purdy's Daniel Haws and ends just as unfortunately. Neville's paranoia is
exacerbated by the arrival of his master's Victorian mother,
Mrs. Lucas, and he threatens to kill the fearless old dragon.
Paradoxically, it is not the threat of death but finding out that
her daughter has been sleeping with her fiancé there that
drives Mrs. Lucas out of the house. Neville returns and sheds
blood all over her abandoned garments as he commits a ritual
sacrifice to her as the blessed Virgin, in his crazed mind asso-
ciating her unbending moral authoritarianism with that of the
Church and his thwarted love for Brendan with the love of
Christ.

Brendan is no Christ, just a member of the foreign service,
a diplomat, a perennial bachelor with what he fears is an in-
cestuous love for his sister, who says she intends to marry his
rather self-centered French friend, Xavier. Once the mother
has disowned her daughter, the daughter feels free to leave
Xavier and pursue her career in ballet.

With Neville dead and Xavier renounced, brother and
sister have successfully stopped the spreading fires of love and
jealousy and have freed themselves of the fear of loss that ac-
companies any close attachment. They are free to pursue their
careers. One may wonder if they have chosen freedom at the
expense of love and *caritas* in their unwillingness to commit
themselves to the welfare of another in need of their love and
compassion, but considering the natures of Neville and Xavier,
it is probably well for their own sanity and sense of self that
they opted for freedom.

This novel goes beyond *Morning in Antibes* to show that
the commitment of love may have too high a price, and it
underscores the reconciliation of the *The Paragon*, substituting

career and self-discipline for the entanglements of love and responsibility.

KEN KESEY

In 1958 Ken Kesey was attending Stanford on a creative-writing scholarship. His parents had emigrated to Oregon from the Southwest in the 1940s. His father had founded a marketing cooperative for dairy farmers in the Willamette valley. Kesey, as his biographer, the journalist Tom Wolfe, describes him, was a product of his father's ambition and affluence.[14] The virtues of his heroes, Randle Patrick McMurphy, in *One Flew Over the Cuckoo's Nest* (1962), and Hank Stamper, in *Sometimes a Great Notion* (1964), are typically those of the virile, self-reliant pioneer who has an unquenchable belief in freedom and his own ability to conquer.

Like the earlier novelist Thomas Wolfe, he adopted a style that depended on what Kesey called "the spew of the diary mind." Unlike Kerouac, however, who also saw the "spew" as the essential raw material of his work, Kesey believes in re-working it so as to accent the "drift" of it without letting the prose seem reworked.[15] Kesey's prose is not "spontaneous," though it may seem so at first glance. His novels have undergone a good deal of revision, although he has always been careful to keep the forward pressure of rapid recall an essential current in his work.

Like Wolfe and Kerouac, Kesey creates heroes who exult in their physical life and the flood of sensations they experience as they move through their environments at a fast pace. Mc-Murphy's initials are R.P.M. and he is in continuous motion, which is not a means of coming to ecstasy as it is for Kerouac's fast-movers but the means by which he avoids being confined to the staticity and order of the Combine that dominates the lives of his fellow inmates in the madhouse. In *Sometimes a Great Notion* Hank Stamper's vitality is what saves him from being forced to accede to the demands of collective organization. He goes it alone, saving not only his own individual freedom but the very ideal of freedom for all the others who would have bowed to the Combine's view that no man can succeed alone.

Like Kerouac, Kesey fueled his consciousness with drugs to aid his precision of images and speed up the pace of their mental projection. Kesey participated in a drug experiment at the Menlo Park Veterans Hospital in 1960 and wrote parts of *Cuckoo's Nest* under the influence of LSD and other psychedelic drugs while working as a night orderly at the same hospital. Just as he controlled the "spew" of his recollections generally, he also controlled what he wrote of his experience under drugs by carefully examining in the normal, conscious state what he had written of his experience under drugs and by going back under the influence of drugs to check on his normal-minded analysis.[16]

In *Cuckoo's Nest* McMurphy wrangles a transfer from a work farm to a psychiatric hospital, where he will, he hopes, find life easier and where he will also find a number of "marks" for his talents as a gambler. When he gets there and he sees that the inmates are being tyrannized over by Big Nurse and the Combine, he becomes sympathetic to the plight of his fellows. Big Nurse is a woman who denies her womanhood, a powerful but sterile matriarch who stifles all individual incentive and censures all individual differences under the collective term "insanity." Kesey's loony bin is very much the American society at large, which is losing its respect for individual freedom while demanding maternal care from the Combines of government, industry, and labor. McMurphy is the rugged individualist who arouses the sadly repressed desires for individual self-realization in the Acutes and the Chronics, who have all but given up hope of reestablishing their unique identities.

McMurphy eventually leads his twelve disciples out of the madhouse and onto a boat to go fishing. In so doing McMurphy is a kind of secular activist Fisher King, more vital than Eliot's, who fishes in a dull canal behind the gashouse in *The Waste Land*, or Kerouac's Jack Duluoz, in a fisherman's waterproof in San Francisco and lost in delirium tremens at Big Sur. Yet, for all his drive and aggressiveness, McMurphy ends up a martyr to his faith in man's potential. Driven past the point of endurance, determined to strike back at the very heart of Big Nurse's heartlessness, he rips open the front of her uniform, exposing her enormous breasts, symbolic of her enormously overweening maternal power. After McMurphy is lobotomized at Big Nurse's instigation, he is very kindly suffocated to death by the schizophrenic narrator, the part-Indian, Chief Broom. Broom then escapes to carry forth the message of hope that McMurphy died to state. The battle against the Combine is never won, but as long as men will fight against it, freedom can be preserved.

During his Stanford University days Kesey was interested in the comic-strip hero as an expression of popular myth. The omnipotence of Superman and Captain Marvel seemed the right heroic expression for a nation successful in peace and war as America had proved itself to be by the end of the 1950s. Kerouac developed the fantasies of *Doctor Sax* from his boyhood reading of *The Shadow* comics; but whereas Doctor Sax, Shadow laugh and all, is not really triumphant in the end, the marvelous McMurphy and the superpowerful Hank Stamper transcend death and defeat on their own merits. In Kerouac the forces of the universe are stronger than the cunning Doctor Sax or the speeding Dean Moriarty. In Kesey nature (the Stampers' river, McMurphy's death) gives way before the vision and drive of the superhero.

In *Cuckoo's Nest* Kesey told his story from the perspective of Chief Broom. In *Sometimes a Great Notion* he tells his story from several points of view, letting us see the several viewpoints of the Stamper family and the labor leaders as well as some of the other loggers and townspeople concerning the strike at the Stamper's lumber mill. The changing points of view are somewhat confusing, but by having all the thoughts and feelings of the others dependent upon the actions of Hank Stamper, a focal center is preserved and the depth and extent of Hank's influence is magnified. Hank Stamper in the world of normal men is twice the hero that McMurphy is in the world of mental misfits. Like Superman, he is alive at the end of this episode to fight against future perils.

When Hank's father, Henry Stamper, went West though others of his family were content to settle in the Midwest, he went determined to "never give an inch." His lifelong acquaintance Boney Stokes has preached all his life that the only way to get along in pioneer country is for men to work together, but Henry has always gone it alone, and now so will his son Hank. The district union organizer, Draeger, believes that Hank will capitulate when he finds out how unloved he becomes as the strike drags on. When his lifelong friend Joe Ben dies while they are trying to move logs by themselves, Hank is tempted to quit; but when the townspeople offer him a Thanksgiving dinner, that bit of welfare kindness is too humiliating. He replies to Draeger and the loggers' demands by hanging his father's amputated arm on the flag pole with all the fingers tied down except the extended middle one, and he and his brother, Leland, take a towboat out to haul their hand-logged logs down to the mill on the flooding river.

Hank is larger than life. He swims the flooded river. He has lost a couple of fingers but is always ready for a fight. He is almost bested by an arch rival, Big Newton, but in the end Hank knocks out Newton's teeth. He thinks of his brother always as "the kid," even after "the kid" has cuckolded him. When he fights with Leland over that event, Leland realizes that his older brother will kill him if he lets him, but only if he lets him. When Leland fights back, he instills in himself the very force that Hank has been waiting to see displayed and gains his self-respect as well as his brother's admiration.

Interestingly enough, when Hank lets down after Joe Ben's death and tells the lumbermen that he is not going to fulfill the contract he has with Wakonda Pacific after all, an act which would defeat the purpose of the strike and presumably keep the men out of work longer, they show him a genuine affection and forgiveness that is nevertheless tainted with a definite feeling of unease. Big Newton regards this new Hank Stamper with a look of sheer terror. When Big Newton hears that Stamper has changed his mind and is towing the logs on the flooded river with only two men to help him, he starts doing pushups. God is back in the competitive swim and all is right with the world. Kesey is telling us that lesser men need their heroes. Without them they lose their identity, their hope, and their freedom. What is more, the hero may not only be one to equal but one to strive against. He is the God to be worshiped only so long as he is strong, only so long as he can stand the trials to which the forces of society and nature and the power drives of other men subject him.

Where Kerouac's all-American hero fails and Kesey's succeeds is in the degree to which they influence the lives of others. Neal-Dean-Cody is ever the irresponsible little boy exulting in his physical prowess, upsetting to his women and his friends but having no real effect outside of this small group of people. Hank Stamper, on the other hand, is the linchpin of his community. He can accomplish his ends alone or with others, but if with others then it must be his way. In the end they are better off with him than against him, for he is, against all the Draegers and Evenwrites and the other collectivists, not only their source of employment but their moral salvation. The way of salvation that Kerouac preaches is ever the way of Old World ecstatic or contemplative mysticism; Kesey's is the more American, secular, pragmatic way of individual free enterprise. Kerouac's answer to man's ills is religious, whereas Kesey's in this book is Promethean.

While working on *Sometimes a Great Notion*, Kesey was using the proceeds from the sale of *Cuckoo's Nest* to buy a six-acre place in San Mateo, where he gathered around him a number of drug-taking characters he called the Merry Pranksters. They traveled around in a psychedelic-colored bus spreading the gospel of "fun, love, and acid." Neal Cassady, fresh out of jail after his marijuana conviction, piloted the bus.[17] Their trip into Mexico in 1966 became the basis of Kesey's screenplay *Over the Border*.[18]

In the screenplay he echoes some of the themes of *Great Notion*. The play begins with a motto: "It is better to fail with faith than to succeed with security. . . ." Devlin Deboree, the philosophic central character, believes we all search for answers to "What makes it go?" and we all want to know "How do I drive it?" At the end of the drama the Voice in the Sky says that when the young American follows up these two questions with "How do I get off?" he flunks the flight school and "concerns our winged way no more." When Deboree fails to try to save his son, Quiston, from being swept away by a wave, the group of Animal Friends, as the Pranksters are called here, vote six to five to abandon him. Sandy-Undine, however, points out that their hopes really rest on the "knucklehead," as she calls their strange guru. They vote for reversal and the film is run backward so that Deboree is given a second chance. He dashes over the cliff this time to a thunderous ovation, and his son's rescue, after pleading: "I'm an American just like any American and I'll use anything I lay my hands on to get me elected President but *that's not me*! Let me try again to be, my God . . . my Lord . . . Whoever. . . ."[19]

Throughout their adventures in Mexico the group has mocked the police, denied authority of all sorts, poked fun at Behema's pregnancy, been careless of childbearing and childrearing, shown little respect for property, and hazarded life and limb in silly joy rides in a wildly painted bus and an old Buick. It takes Quiston's "death" to bring them to their senses. The six-to-five vote is ambiguous but Deboree's repentance and their response to it is not. From the depths of absurdity they are rescued by a rearousal of the old heroic values of unflinching courage and certain love. With these values he accomplishes the impossible, and Quiston (mankind perhaps) is saved. American opportunism is renounced and the higher American ideal of heroic self-realization is affirmed.

In 1966 and 1967 Kesey was sponsoring LSD parties in the Haight-Ashbury section of San Francisco.[20] He said later that Timothy Leary, leading LSD guru of the period, was his own personal "turn-on." In *The Electric Kool-Aid Acid Test* Tom Wolfe describes Kesey as the leader of the Pranksters at the Trips Festival in San Francisco in the mid-sixties. He is shown throughout the book as the charismatic leader of a group of acid freaks. Kesey's goal seems to be to create a mass mystical experience for his followers. According to Wolfe, he had the hope of merging the self with Now, of losing the subjective-objective dualism of our normal waking consciousness in the creation of the moment so that what is perceived and what is happening are one and the same at the same time (pp. 288–289). Were this possible, it would mean that a person could become one with the ongoing process of creation. In *Over the Border* Deboree at the seashore tries by the hour to let himself move with the ocean waves in an attempt to become synchronous with the forces of nature. He is convinced that if there is to be a revolution in man's thought that it must come through a merging with the life forces, that there is no way to successfully go against the waves. The trick is to put oneself "in synch." His salvation, however, lies not in passive receptivity but in heroic action, rescuing his son, against all the obvious natural odds. In the rearousal of the philosopher's basic animal, paternal instincts he taps certain elemental forces (going with the waves) that enable him to succeed, as Hank Stamper succeeds in swimming the flooded river to confront his brother seducing his wife. "Heroism is natural if we let it be" seems to be Kesey's motto.

When Kesey and Paul Krassner decided to edit *The Last Supplement to the Whole Earth Catalog*, Kesey incorporated some of his own essays written during the late 1960s. In these essays he offers certain "tools" to the reader for a satisfying life. Among these is the Bible, which he says he has found most useful since his son's near-death, when in desperation he prayed and realized that he was indeed fortunate in knowing *"where* to call." He also suggests the use of the I-Ching as a way of putting the conscious mind in touch with the subconscious truth, the use of ginseng to restore tranquility, and the use of marijuana in lieu of impure LSD. He quotes Martin Buber and speaks of a revolution of the heart. Like Kerouac, he has also said that he does not believe in social revolution. Revolutionaries are dishonest, he says. What is honest is one man's feeling for another specific individual and his own feelings about himself.[21]

Kesey's superheroes have not learned, as Wolfe's George Webber did, that no man can devour the earth or, as Jack Duluoz did, that the drive to heroism and Godhead ends in lonely disillusion. Kesey's view is vital, youthful, feeding on its own success, believing in the power of the human will over all else. As a statement of feeling and belief, *Sometimes a Great Notion* is in its own way as heady a piece of literature as Emerson's "Self-Reliance," and just as dangerous.

The danger is that absolute, independent freedom of the Stamper variety subjugates the weaker to the stronger in such a fashion that only the strongest can have such freedom and only at the expense of all others it controls. As Arthur Miller put it, by Kesey's standards Charles Manson, the mass murderer, "becomes an ambiguous villain, for he went the whole way, and if repression is the only enemy then Charley was incarnate liberation."[22]

Kesey's characterizations in *Sometimes a Great Notion* indicate the simplistic *laissez-faire* philosophy at the base of the work. The collectivists, Evenwrite and Draeger, are either cowardly sneaks (Evenwrite) or polite theoreticians without force (Draeger). When Joe Ben dies pinned under a log in a rising river, he dies with stoic, laughing grace only because he believes in God and Hank Stamper. When Viv leaves Hank, after lying with his younger brother, she leaves to have a life of her own. One might say that she should leave out of shame, but that is not the case. One might say that Hank should bring her back, but that is not the case. Kesey seems to be saying that we all need to be left on our own and that we will all profit from independence. The misery of the company town is not brought on by the greed of its townspeople but by a reasonable desire for a greater share of the wealth they help to produce. They have not lost the battle at the end of the book but are waiting the outcome of Hank Stamper's last daring move in fear and awe. Kesey suggests that if the loggers win the strike and Hank is vanquished they will all be moral losers, as the virtue of individual self-reliance is submerged under the rising tide of welfare-collectivism.

Kesey's hero is at once a simplistic exponent of rugged individualism and deeply American. He is part of a lasting current in American thought, unlike Kerouac's Neal-Dean-Cody, who is a kind of perversion of the principles since his individualism builds nothing, defeats nothing, goes nowhere, and commands little respect outside his own group of dropouts. Kerouac operates on the fringe of American society, but Kesey is right in the midstream in the deepest current, albeit weaker than it was in the time of Emerson and Whitman. With the admission in *Doctor Sax* that evil is not really a husk of doves, that it is very real and that only the godly forces in the universe which are beyond man's conscious will can exterminate it, Kerouac eliminates the possibilities of a superhero. His recourse is to mysticism. Kesey's heroes move mountains with faith in themselves and the Protestant ethic. They appeal to our blood and our image of the American dream, while at the same time they appear a little silly, like Doctor Sax conjuring away the rising forces of evil with his worthless powders.

8

The Duluoz Legend
in Perspective

AMONG THE WRITERS just discussed, Kerouac's vision of life appears to be the most despairing. In the end Salinger is committing his characters to "do it for the Fat Lady," to be what they can be according to the talents they possess and to do the best they can for themselves and for the rest of not-so-fortunate mankind. Purdy's characters despair of finding an authoritative center to their existence, and several of them perish for lack of it; but the burden of the later works by Purdy is that in a life without absolutes honest, human *caritas* is all-important. Purdy's urgent explorations of the tangled and torturous web of love in *The Nephew, Eustace Chisholm*, and *Jeremy's Version* remain man-centered to the end. In Kerouac the relationships of characters are always secondary to the individual quest for Godhead.

In Knowles and Kesey the individual is in pursuit of his own freedom to become whatever he can, and in this respect his reach toward heroism is not unlike that of Kerouac's Sal Paradise, Jack Duluoz, and Neal-Dean-Cody. But whereas Kerouac's heroes are not satisfied with anything less than apotheosis and tend to give all experience en route short shrift, Knowles's Gene Forrester learns that it cannot be so, Cleet

Kinsolving sees success in earthly terms, and Lou Colfax and Brendan Lucas escape the entanglements of sexual love not through mysticism but through devotion to their careers. Kesey's McMurphy learns to love the men he was going to bilk, and Hank Stamper is so loving that he can forgive his wife's leaving and his brother's hate. Devlin Deboree too comes to his senses in time to know that responsibility for human life is more important than theological experimentation.

When we look at Kerouac in context with these other writers, it is easy to see that mysticism took him farther beyond the struggle with everyday life than it did any of the others. The tenacity with which he held to his vision of the Golden Eternity is a measure of the degree to which the world disgusted him. It was simply not worthwhile to try to understand it in detail or come to terms with it. It was in itself too imperfect.

Kerouac's is the most despairing view of all because he has set his sights the highest and fallen the farthest short and because he has steadfastly refused to compromise with the world's imperfection. He has set the limits to visionary idealism through his own experience writ large in the autobiographical fiction of the Duluoz Legend. It is, in fact, within the limits that he defined that the others have their own expression.

His disgust and its outlet in mysticism turned him away from any careful consideration of the manners of our society. He develops few solid characters and few memorable scenes in which characters interact in meaningful dialogue. What he does do well through characterization is to show us the vagaries of a sensitive and impressionable mind deeply disturbed by the postwar malaise.

We have seen his view of primal innocence reflected in the child characters of young Jack Duluoz, Ti Jean, and Gerard and in Kerouac's treatment of primitive peoples, outcasts, and unspoiled nature. He makes innocence a virtue and tries in the ministrations of Doctor Sax and the devotions of Memère to suggest that a blind and simple faith that life will work out is to be preferred to getting entangled in its complexities and doing battle with it on its own terms. To escape this entanglement requires the utmost spontaneity and general freedom of action. For this purpose, the "road" becomes not only an escape but a route of preservation, a route, however, that inescapably leads back to the maladjusted self and to despair.

In Kerouac the mother is the symbol of life's certitude and durability, the father the emblem of uncertainty and death. The tie to the mother keeps the Kerouac persona from a normal sexual attachment to other women, and the distrust of the father leads to a profound distrust of his father's world. Kerouac seeks release in mysticism and nature from the demands of the father's brick-walled, city world. There is also, through a succession of novels, a struggle to reconcile instinctive sexual need with religious propriety, a reconciliation finally achieved in *Big Sur*, the last of the Beat novels, though not the last Kerouac work.

The boyhood heroic vision of the author is fictionalized in *Doctor Sax* and other Lowell novels. His view of the writer as hero is paralleled by his quest for a great American hero for his fiction, the prototype of which he thought he had found in Neal Cassady. Cassady's energy and spontaneity fascinated Kerouac, and he came to think of him as "a new kind of American saint" with the stamina and strength of mind to create a revolution in American life. Together, they sought to lead the way to spiritual transcendence through a quest for ecstasy. Their method was to collapse and intensify the normal processes of time through a rush of sensations, brought about by fast action and the stimulation of the senses through the use of drugs and alcohol. Jazz and sex also abet the intensity. The quest for ecstasy results, however, not in enlightenment but in an indiscriminating blur of sensations; and the hero shows himself to be a victim of his fear of failure in a land where the American dream is no longer tenable.

Kerouac's characters are separated from the community and have no interest in social reorganization, much to the disgust of many of the author's critics. But to the Kerouac hero the world and its institutions are too absurd for personal involvement. Nature offers no lasting relief either. Essentially, it is blind and uncaring. The only answer seems to be to get beyond time and desire, either through annihilating the senses with sensation or by freezing them in mystic contemplation. Neither method is satisfactory, and Kerouac's focal characters oscillate endlessly between the two states until, with the publication of the last novel, *Vanity of Duluoz*, it is evident that the quest for ecstasy and oneness with God has perpetuated an incorrigible loneliness, the final position of the quintessential Beat.

What relief there is in mystical belief is due to Kerouac's study of Buddhism superimposed upon his early Catholic training. He longs to accept the dance of life, the play of the illusion that most consider their waking reality, while at the same time seeking contact with the spiritual center of existence. He identifies himself with the Mahayana Buddhist and eschews the more fashionable and more socially active way of Zen. He also denies the possibility of reincarnation, holding rather to his early child's view of heaven, the Golden Eternity. His statement that at heart he is really an old-fashioned Catholic mystic, his fear of women as a source of temptation that keeps men from knowing God, his one year's practice of chastity prior to the experiences in *Dharma Bums*, and his periodic withdrawals into solitude manifest his monklike rejection of the postwar world. Had the rejection been more complete or had he been able to find a religious mode of reconciliation, Kerouac might have finished his work more beatifically than Beat; but the Duluoz Legend, in the final analysis, is the saga of Beatness, of man stranded between an unsatisfactory world and an untenable heaven, somewhere in the void.

Fascinated by the play of his own mind, Kerouac tried to get down all of his experience into words, first in the manner of Thomas Wolfe and then more in the manner of Henry Miller and William Burroughs. The "Tape" section of *Visions of*

Cody represents one extreme, and *The Subterraneans* the other. His theory of Spontaneous Prose developed out of his understanding of jazz and experimentation akin to that of the Black Mountain poets. His poetry is generally vapid, his prose uneven, but the best of it has a nervous intensity that gives the method value. It is particularly well suited to Kerouac's essentially confessional mode of utterance.

He has left us a body of work including the novels of the Duluoz Legend, his poetry, and his long unpublished treatise on Buddhism, but it is probable that little of it will survive. Because of continuing interest in the Beat generation, *On the Road* will no doubt remain the novel to be read to get at the quintessence of Beatness. Complementary works on the Beats will also retain a certain appeal. *Dharma Bums* contains some of the memorable minor characters, such as Japhy Ryder and Sean Monahan, and some of the best description of nature. It also treats the hero's mystic quest with the greatest degree of detachment. *Big Sur* is the novel that sums up the futility of Beat existence.

Whatever the merits of Spontaneous Prose, and we might wish for prose better honed or more thoroughly revised in a number of his books, Kerouac's prose method did produce at least one remarkable book, *The Subterraneans*, in which the spontaneity of style is largely responsible for the strength of its effect. It is a novel that is unique in its intensity, not only in all of Kerouac's work but in the work of the New Romantics generally.

The Lowell novels are not particularly remarkable, with the exception of *Doctor Sax*, which contains some wonderful descriptions of boyhood fancies that shape the course of a man's desires. Kerouac is right that his first novel, *The Town and the City*, is dead. It is a rather labored effort, and the Martin family is no more interesting than the fictional families of a number of other authors working in that mode. *Vanity of Duluoz* fares no better, although it is a quite thorough reworking of the material of the earlier novel.

The rest, *Visions of Cody, Visions of Gerard, Tristessa, Maggie Cassidy, Pic,* and all the other stories and the poetry are most likely ephemeral. Nevertheless, five worthwhile novels is a singular achievement for any author. He will be remembered as the king of the Beats for his vision of Beatness and his chronicles of personal *angst,* and when prose style is discussed, his ideas of Spontaneous Prose will appear afresh. As a keeper of the innocent vision and as one who held it tenaciously against the pressures of reconciliation with a corrupt world, he will be remembered as the Jeremiah-like prophet of post–World War II Romanticism.

Notes

THE FIRST TIME a work is referred to, I have given full documentation in a note. Subsequent references are cited parenthetically in the text.

1

THE CHILD'S INNOCENT VISION

1. *Vanity of Duluoz* (New York: Coward-McCann, Inc., 1967), p. 195.
2. Kerouac quoted in Allen Ginsberg, "The Great Rememberer," *Saturday Review*, 2 Dec. 1972, p. 60. This essay was later revised and issued as a preface to Kerouac's *Visions of Cody*.
3. Bruce Cook, *The Beat Generation* (New York: Charles Scribner's Sons, 1971), p. 78.
4. Ann Charters, *Kerouac* (San Francisco: Straight Arrow Press, 1973), pp. 161–167.
5. *Doctor Sax* (New York: Grove Press, Inc., 1959), p. 17.
6. *Lonesome Traveler* (New York: McGraw-Hill Book Co., Inc., 1960), pp. 34–36.
7. *On the Road* (New York: The Viking Press, 1957), p. 124.
8. *Tristessa* (New York: Avon Books, 1960), p. 41.
9. *The Town and the City* (New York: Harcourt, Brace and Company, 1950), p. 424.

10. *Visions of Gerard* (New York: Farrar, Straus and Co., 1963), pp. 48–50.
11. See Ann Charters, *A Bibliography of Works by Jack Kerouac, 1939–1967* (New York: Phoenix, 1967), p. 20. In a conversation with Kerouac about his book of poetry, *The Scripture of the Golden Eternity*, Kerouac is quoted as saying, "I'm a Catholic all along. I was really kidding Gary Snyder." Snyder was fictionalized as Japhy Ryder, student of Buddhism, in the earlier *Dharma Bums*.
12. "Jack Kerouac Comes Home," *Atlantic*, July 1965, p. 71.
13. *Desolation Angels* (New York: Coward-McCann, Inc., 1965), p. 152.
14. See Salinger's *Raise High the Roof Beam, Carpenters* and *Seymour, an Introduction*.
15. In *A Casebook on the Beat*, ed. Thomas Parkinson (New York: Thomas Y. Crowell Co., 1961), p. 207.
16. "Manhattan Sketches," in *The Moderns*, ed. Le Roi Jones (New York: Corinth Books, 1963), p. 274.
17. *Pic* (New York: Grove Press, Inc., 1971), p. 69.
18. In Parkinson, ed., *Casebook*, pp. 32–33. This sketch originally appeared in *Evergreen Review* 1, No. 2 (1957):119–136.
19. "Kerouac's *The Subterraneans*," *Mainstream* 15, No. 6 (1958): 62.
20. *The Subterraneans* (New York: Grove Press, Inc., 1958), p. 67.
21. "The Time of the Geek" (a reprinted section of *The Town and the City*), in *Protest*, eds. Gene Feldman and Max Gartenberg (London: Souvenir, 1959), p. 82.
22. "Rumbling, Rambling Blues," *Playboy*, Jan. 1958, pp. 57, 71–72.
23. *The Dharma Bums* (New York: New American Library, 1959), p. 127.
24. In Jones, ed., *The Moderns*, pp. 250–265.
25. *Big Sur* (New York: Farrar, Straus, and Cudahy, 1962), p. 17.
26. *Visions of Cody* (New York: McGraw-Hill Book Company, 1972), p. 26.

2

FATHER DEATH AND MOTHER EARTH

1. *Book of Dreams* (San Francisco: City Lights Books, 1961), p. 155.
2. Charters, *Kerouac*, pp. 64–65.
3. *Maggie Cassidy* (New York: Avon Books, 1959), p. 153.
4. *Mexico City Blues* (New York: Grove Press, Inc., 1959), p. 103.
5. A satiric attack on the Freudians occurs in the 175th Chorus of *Mexico City Blues*, p. 175. In a letter to Allen Ginsberg, dated July 1958, he says, "Me for midnight silence, and morning freshness, and afternoon clouds, and my own kind of Lowell boy life. As for the Freudian implications, or Marxian, or Reichian or Spenglerian, I'll buy Beethoven." This letter is contained in the Ginsberg Collection at Columbia University.
6. John Montgomery, *A Memoir of Jack Kerouac* (Fresno: Giligia Press, 1970), p. 9.
7. In *The Twelfth Anniversary Playboy Reader*, ed. Hugh Hefner (Chicago: Playboy Press, 1965), pp. 638–649.
8. In Jones, ed., *The Moderns*, pp. 250–265.

3

THE AMERICAN HERO QUEST

1. Preface to *Excerpts from Visions of Cody* (New York: New Directions, 1959).
2. Kerouac, Jack, "The Origins of the Beat Generation," in Parkinson, ed., *Casebook*, p. 74.
3. Ibid., pp. 70 and 75.
4. Cook, *Beat Generation*, p. 204.
5. *Satori in Paris* (New York: Grove Press, Inc., 1966), p. 28.
6. In Parkinson, ed., *Casebook*, pp. 72–73.
7. "The White Negro," in *Man in Crisis*, ed. Joseph K. Davis (New York: Scott, Foresman and Co., 1970), p. 392.
8. "The White Negro," in Davis, ed., *Man in Crisis*, p. 391.
9. Paul Goodman, *Growing up Absurd* (New York: Random House, 1960), p. 185.

10. In Davis, ed., *Man in Crisis*, p. 391.
11. Lawrence Lipton, *The Holy Barbarians* (New York: Julian Messner, 1959), pp. 158–159.
12. See "The Railroad Earth," in *Lonesome Traveler*, pp. 37–83.
13. Charters, *Works by Jack Kerouac*, p. 25.

4

ACCEPTING LOSTNESS FOREVER

1. "The Great Rememberer," *Saturday Review*, 2 Dec. 1972, p. 62.
2. "Disengagement: The Art of the Beat Generation," in Parkinson, ed., *Casebook*, p. 193.
3. "The Know-Nothing Bohemians," ibid., p. 211.
4. "The Beat Generation," *New Statesman*, 23 Aug. 1958, p. 294.
5. "Joan Rawshanks in the Fog," *Transatlantic Review*, Spring 1962, pp. 57–72. This sketch also appears as part of *Visions of Cody*.
6. In Jones, ed., *The Moderns*, pp. 244–249.
7. 211th Chorus of *Mexico City Blues*, p. 211.
8. "James Jones and Jack Kerouac: Novelists of Disjunction," in *The Creative Present*, eds. Nona Balekian and Charles Simmons (Garden City: Doubleday and Company, 1963), p. 208.
9. "Quests, Cars, and Kerouac," *University of Kansas City Review* 28 (1962):238–239.
10. John Clellon Holmes, *Nothing More to Declare* (New York: E. P. Dutton and Co., Inc., 1967), p. 107.

5

THE GOLDEN ETERNITY

1. Charters, *Kerouac*, pp. 200–209. In May 1954 Kerouac wrote Ginsberg a fourteen-page letter in which he recommended various texts for the poet's study of Buddhism. In it he also refers to a hundred-page introductory essay that he has written which he calls "Some of the Dharma." This letter is contained in the Ginsberg Collection at Columbia University.

2. Scripture #11, *The Scripture of the Golden Eternity* (New York: Corinth Books, 1970), p. 21.
3. "The Origins of the Beat Generation," in Parkinson, ed., *Casebook*, pp. 69–70.
4. Ginsberg Collection, Columbia University.
5. 108 Chorus of *Mexico City Blues*.
6. "Beat Zen, Square Zen, and Zen," in *The World of Zen*, ed. Nancy Wilson Ross (New York: Vintage Books, 1960), pp. 334–335.

6

SPONTANEOUS PROSE

1. Cook, *Beat Generation*, p. 66.
2. Charters, *Works by Jack Kerouac*, p. 4.
3. Introduction to *Lonesome Traveler*, pp. iv–v.
4. *Newsweek*, 13 March 1950, pp. 80 and 82.
5. Chicago *Sun-Tribune*, 5 March 1950, p. 4.
6. See Richard S. Kennedy, *The Window of Memory: The Literary Career of Thomas Wolfe* (Chapel Hill: University of North Carolina Press, 1962).
7. *New York Times Book Review*, 18 Feb. 1968, p. 4.
8. "In Loving Memory of Myself," *Saturday Review*, 5 July 1959, p. 23.
9. "King of the Beats," *Commonweal* 69 (1959):359–360.
10. "*The Dharma Bums*," in *The Village Voice Reader*, eds. Daniel Wolf and Edwin Fancher (New York: Doubleday & Company, Inc., 1962), pp. 340–342.
11. Quoted in Cook, *Beat Generation*, from Kerouac's essay "Essentials of Spontaneous Prose," p. 73.
12. "Essentials of Spontaneous Prose," in Parkinson, ed., *Casebook*, pp. 65–67.
13. Charters, *Works by Jack Kerouac*, p. 8.
14. Ibid., p. 27.
15. "The Blazing and the Beat," *Time*, 24 Feb. 1958, p. 104.
16. Quoted in Charters, *Works by Jack Kerouac*, p. 9.
17. Introduction to *Desolation Angels*.

18. "Old Angel Midnight Part Two," *Evergreen Review*, Aug.–Sept. 1964, pp. 68–71.
19. See Cook, *Beat Generation*, pp. 1–17.
20. Krim, Introduction to *Desolation Angels*, p. xi.
21. "Disengagement: The Art of the Beat Generation," in Parkinson, ed., *Casebook*, pp. 182–183.
22. "Book Burners and Sweet Sixteen," *Saturday Review*, 27 June 1959, pp. 22 and 30.
23. Mailer is quoted at length in Clancy Sigal, "Nihilism's Organization Man," *Universities and Left Review*, Summer 1958, pp. 59–65.
24. Kerouac, preface to *Scattered Poems* (San Francisco: City Lights Books, 1970).
25. See E. E. Cummings, *i: six nonlectures* (Cambridge: Harvard University Press, 1954).
26. "Disengagement: The Art of the Beat Generation," in Parkinson, ed., *Casebook*, p. 181.
27. "A Translation from the French of Jean-Louis Incogniteau," *Scattered Poems*, unpaged.
28. Charters, *Kerouac*, pp. 139–292.
29. Letter to Ginsberg, 13 Nov. 1945. In the Ginsberg Collection at Columbia University.
30. "(An Imaginary Portrait of Ulysses S. Grant/Edgar Allen Poe)," an unpaginated pamphlet in the U.C.L.A. Special Collections, written c. 1957.
31. Charters, *Kerouac*, p. 361.
32. "*Beat Generation?* Dead as Davy Crockett Caps, Says Rexroth Passing Through," in Wolf and Fancher, eds., *The Village Voice Reader*, p. 338.
33. "The Know-Nothing Bohemians," in Parkinson, ed., *Casebook*, p. 204.
34. Review of *On the Road*, in *Midstream*, Winter 1958, reprinted as Appendix E in Goodman, *Growing up Absurd*, p. 280.
35. "Hip, Cool, Beat and Frantic," *Nation*, 16 Nov. 1957, pp. 354–355.
36. "*The Dharma Bums*," in Wolf and Fancher, eds., *The Village Voice Reader*, p. 343

7

THE NEW ROMANTICISM

1. *J. D. Salinger* (New York: Twayne Publishers, 1963), passim.
2. "Between Miracle and Suicide," in *Salinger, a Critical and Personal Portrait*, ed. H. A. Grunwald (New York: Harper and Row, 1962), pp. 176–191.
3. In a letter to Alan Ansen, 20 Aug. 1957, Kerouac expresses his flight from one extreme to the other as follows: "Maya my ass, I say—Wisdom is okay but I want Goethe passion again, 'pathway to wisdom through excess' so at least I can laugh, or cry, or do something, anything but this blank, bleak wonder. . . . Wha'm I gonna do with essence when I got all this matter to carry around on my backlegs? . . . so much cover-up of the fact we dont really know what to do with ourselves—" Contained in the Ginsberg Collection at Columbia University.
4. "Beatific Signals," in Grunwald, ed., *Salinger, a Critical and Personal Portrait*, pp. 165–166.
5. "The Rare Quixotic Gesture," in ibid., p. 147.
6. "Seventy-eight Bananas," in ibid., pp. 123–136.
7. See *Raise High the Roof Beam, Carpenters* and *Seymour, an Introduction*.
8. See also David L. Stevenson, "The Mirror of Crisis," in Grunwald, ed., *Salinger, a Critical and Personal Portrait*, pp. 36–41.
9. *The Not-Right House* (Columbia: University of Missouri Press, 1968), p. 3.
10. See also Thomas Lorch, "Purdy's *Malcolm*: A Unique Vision of Radical Emptiness," *Wisconsin Studies in Contemporary Literature* 6 (1965):204–213.
11. The title of Knowles's book refers to Hemingway's *In Our Time*, chapter six, where the wounded Nick Adams says to Rinaldi that they are not patriots, that they made their separate peace when the war became unbearable. Like Hemingway, Knowles uses code heroes, like Phineas in *A Separate Peace* and Jeannot in *Morning in Antibes*, to show the initiate the way to deal with crisis.
12. *English Journal* 58 (1969):1323–1329.

13. *Double Vision* (New York: The Macmillan Company, 1964), pp. 206–211.

14. See *The Electric Kool-Aid Acid Test* (New York: Farrar, Straus, 1968).

15. In a letter to Ken Babbs, printed in *One Flew Over the Cuckoo's Nest*, ed. John C. Pratt (New York: The Viking Press, 1973), p. 339.

16. *Kesey's Garage Sale* (New York: The Viking Press, 1973), p. 7.

17. Cook, *Beat Generation*, pp. 197–198.

18. In *Kesey's Garage Sale*, pp. 33–169.

19. *Over the Border*, p. 168.

20. Cook, *Beat Generation*, p. 200.

21. In *Kesey's Garage Sale*, pp. 175–192.

22. Introduction to *Kesey's Garage Sale*, p. xviii.

Index

"The White Negro" (Mailer), 40
Whitman, Walt, 63
"Why Can't They Tell You Why"
    (Purdy), 108
Williams, William Carlos, 80, 88.
    See also Black Mountain Poets

Wolfe, Thomas, 1, 23, 42, 76–77,
    78, 93, 119, 121, 134
Wolfe, Tom, 127

You Can't Go Home Again
    (Wolfe), 78